Amazing Grace

# *Amazing Grace*

## Hymn Texts for Devotional Use

Bert Polman, Marilyn Kay Stulken,
and James Rawlings Sydnor, editors

Westminster John Knox Press
Louisville, Kentucky

© 1994 Westminster John Knox Press

*Book and cover design by Drew Stevens*

*First edition*

Published by Westminster John Knox Press
Louisville, Kentucky

This book is printed on acid-free paper that meets the American National Standards Institute Z39.48 standard. ♾

PRINTED IN THE UNITED STATES OF AMERICA

   95 96 97 98 99 00 01 02 03 — 10 9 8 7 6 5 4 3 2

**Library of Congress Cataloging-in-Publication Data**

Amazing grace : hymn texts for devotional use / Bert Polman, Marilyn
   Kay Stulken, James Rawlings Sydnor, editors.
        p.   cm.
   Includes index.
   ISBN 0-664-25510-8 (alk. paper)
     1. Hymns—Devotional use.    I. Polman, Bertus Frederick.
II. Stulken, Marilyn Kay, date.    III. Sydnor, James Rawlings.
BV340.A48    1994
245—dc20                                                   94-28794

# Contents

## HOLY SPIRIT

## CHRISTIAN LIFE

# Preface

Hymn texts should be our companions in daily life. This can only occur if we have them lodged in our memory or available in a handy volume that will fit in our pocket, purse, or traveling bag. Therefore the texts of some of the best hymns of Christendom are published in this compact volume.

For most Christians, contact with hymns is limited to a few minutes of singing in Sunday morning worship. Although the words of hymns can be understood while they are sung, it is a fact that hymns can be comprehended in greater depth when the texts are read before they are sung.

One of America's leading hymnologists, Louis Fitz-Gerald Benson (1855–1930), wrote: "Hymns that are not made personally familiar by devotional reading have not much spiritual influence. . . . It is only the precedent appropriation of the hymn's message by each individual heart that makes its congregational singing worthwhile."

Most present-day hymnal publishers issue their books in a format designed to facilitate congregational singing. Therefore they include both text and music, usually with the words interlined between music staves. This is an appropriate format for use in corporate worship in that it places words and music adjacent to each other. However, for devotional reading, the hymns should be printed in poetic form instead of being placed within the music.

These hymns can also be sung in one's private devotions. John Calvin said that there are two types of prayers. "Some are uttered by word alone, the others with song." Because many of these texts have different tunes in various denominational hymnals, we have not indicated a tune name. But for most of them we have noted the meter of the text so that a suitable tune can be found.

In this book the assuring truths of our faith are printed in clear memorable poetry. The authors have written their spiritual autobiographies. They offer their prayers and give commentaries on their faith. Some versify the Scripture. For example, the anonymous author of "How firm a foundation" places quotation marks around the stanzas. Here is the versification of Isaiah 41:10:

> "Fear not, I am with thee, O be not dismayed,
> For I am thy God and will still give thee aid;
> I'll strengthen and help thee, and cause thee to stand,
> Upheld by my righteous, omnipotent hand."

This volume is really a home hymnal instead of being a part of the church pew furnishings. Benson explains it this way: "So inspiring and uplifting can the spiritual ministry of poetry and music to human lives be made that I venture to propose this task and opportunity of getting the hymnal back into the homes and hands and hearts of Christian people as one of the most rewarding that can engage us."

Erik Routley also emphasized the desirability of hymnals in homes: "A man or woman who has one hymnal in the house, and who opens it occasionally, is already on the way to becoming an intelligent hymn singer. . . . I did in my own youth know seniors who kept their hymnal next to their Bible, read from both at their prayers, and snatched both if they were suddenly taken to hospital."

The Hymn Society in the United States and Canada endorsed and recommended the publication of this hymnal. Its Executive Committee appointed the volume's editors. Dr. Bert Polman, member of the Christian Reformed Church, is a professor at Redeemer College, Ancaster, Ontario, Canada. He is the primary author of the handbook to the *Psalter Hymnal*. Dr. Marilyn Kay Stulken, a Lutheran from Racine, Wisconsin, has written the *Hymnal Companion to the Lutheran Book of Worship* and co-authored the companion to the Roman Catholic hymnal *Worship* (Third Edition). Dr. James Rawlings Sydnor, a Presbyterian and a Fellow of the Hymn Society, is emeritus professor of the Presbyterian School of Christian Education, Richmond, Virginia. He has written *Introducing a New Hymnal* and *Hymns and Their Uses* and has either edited or been on editorial committees of seven national hymnals.

A wide variety of hymnals, both denominational and nondenominational, served as resources for this volume. These hymnals represent an equally wide variety of editorial styles and policies in terms of textual alterations, particularly changes for modernized and/or inclusive language. The editors of this present collection have chosen a conservative approach, preferring where possible original hymns or translations and retaining only those alterations that preserved the poetic integrity of the hymns (or in some cases actually improved them). While modern hymnals often indicate textual changes with "alt.," the present editors have not done so with the alterations or revisions of texts and translations in this volume.

The editors express gratitude to scores of owners of hymn copyrights who gave free permission to include their property in this collection. Especially we thank George Shorney, who made available at no cost a large number of hymns for which Hope Publishing Company is the copyright agent. We regret that we could not include a few excellent hymns because the owners asked for fees that we could not afford or placed unacceptable publishing restrictions on their hymns.

The Hymn Society is grateful to the Presbyterian Association of Musicians for contributing to the editorial costs of this volume.

> Bert Polman
> Marilyn Kay Stulken
> James Rawlings Sydnor

# We All Believe in One True God

Apostles' Creed                                        8.7.7.7.7.7
Vers. Tobias Clausnitzer (1668)
Trans. Catherine Winkworth (1863)

We all believe in one true God,
Father, Son, and Holy Ghost,
Ever-present help in need,
Praised by all the heavenly host,
By whose mighty power alone
All is made and wrought and done.

We all believe in Jesus Christ,
Son of God and Mary's son,
Who descended from his throne
And for us salvation won,
By whose cross and death are we
Rescued from sin's misery.

We all confess the Holy Ghost,
Who from both fore'er proceeds,
Who upholds and comforts us
In all trials, fears, and needs.
Blest and Holy Trinity,
Praise forever be to thee!

## All Glory Be to God on High

*Gloria in excelsis*                                        8.7.8.7.8.8.7
Vers. Nikolaus Decius (1541)
Trans. Catherine Winkworth (1863)

All glory be to God on high,
Who hath our race befriended;
To us no harm shall now come nigh,
The strife at last is ended;
God showeth his goodwill to men,
And peace shall reign on earth again;
O thank him for his goodness.

We praise, we worship thee, we trust,
And give thee thanks forever,
O Father, that thy rule is just
And wise, and changes never;
Thy boundless power o'er all things reigns,
Thou dost whate'er thy will ordains:
'Tis well thou art our Ruler!

O Jesus Christ, our God and Lord,
Begotten of the Father,
Who hast our fallen race restored
And straying sheep dost gather,
Thou Lamb of God, enthroned on high,
Behold our need, and hear our cry:
Have mercy on us, Jesus!

O Holy Spirit, precious Gift,
Thou Comforter unfailing,
Do thou our troubled souls uplift,
Against the foe prevailing;
Since Christ for us his blood hath shed,
Avert our woes and calm our dread;
We trust in thee to help us!

# Come, Thou Almighty King

*Collection of Hymns*                                    6.6.4.6.6.6.4
  *for Social Worship* (1757)

Come, thou Almighty King,
Help us thy name to sing,
Help us to praise:
Father, all-glorious,
O'er all victorious,
Come, and reign over us,
Ancient of Days,

Come, thou Incarnate Word,
Gird on thy mighty sword,
Our prayer attend:
Come, and thy people bless,
And give thy word success;
Spirit of holiness,
On us descend.

Come, Holy Comforter,
Thy sacred witness bear
In this glad hour:
Thou who almighty art,
Now rule in every heart,
And ne'er from us depart,
Spirit of power.

To thee, great One in three,
The highest praises be,
Hence evermore!
Thy sovereign majesty
May we in glory see,
And to eternity
Love and adore.


## Father Most Holy

Latin (10th cent.)                                      11.11.11.5
Trans. Percy Dearmer (1906)

Father most holy, merciful, and tender;
Jesus, our Savior, with the Father reigning;
Spirit of comfort, advocate, defender,
Light never waning.

Trinity blessed, unity unshaken;
Goodness unbounded, very God of heaven,
Light of the angels, joy of those forsaken,
Hope of all living.

Maker of all things, all thy creatures praise thee;
All for thy worship were and are created;
Now, as we also worship thee devoutly,
Hear thou our voices.

Lord God Almighty, unto thee be glory,
One in three Persons, over all exalted!
Glory we offer, praise thee and adore thee,
Now and forever.

# Creating God, Your Fingers Trace

Jeffery Rowthorn (1979)                                              LM
                                                              Psalm 148

Creating God, your fingers trace
The bold designs of farthest space;
Let sun and moon and stars and light
And what lies hidden praise your might.

Sustaining God, your hands uphold
Earth's mysteries known or yet untold;
Let water's fragile blend with air,
Enabling life, proclaim your care.

Redeeming God, your arms embrace
All now despised for creed or race;
Let peace, descending like a dove,
Make known on earth your healing love.

Indwelling God, your gospel claims
One family with a billion names;
Let every life be touched by grace
Until we praise you face to face.

# Holy, Holy, Holy! Lord God Almighty!

Reginald Heber (publ. 1827)                                  11.12.12.10
                                                    Revelation 4:8–11

Holy, holy, holy! Lord God Almighty!
Early in the morning our song shall rise to thee,
Holy, holy, holy! merciful and mighty!
God in three Persons, blessed Trinity!

Holy, holy, holy! All the saints adore thee,
Casting down their golden crowns around the glassy sea;
Cherubim and seraphim falling down before thee,
Who wert, and art, and evermore shalt be.

Holy, holy, holy! Though the darkness hide thee,
Though the eye of sinfulness thy glory may not see,
Only thou art holy; there is none beside thee
Perfect in power, in love and purity.

Holy, holy, holy! Lord God Almighty!
All thy works shall praise thy name, in earth and sky and
    sea;
Holy, holy, holy! merciful and mighty!
God in three Persons, blessed Trinity!

# I Bind unto Myself Today

Attr. St. Patrick (5th cent.)
Trans. Cecil Frances Alexander (1889)

I bind unto myself today
The strong name of the Trinity
By invocation of the same,
The Three in One and One in Three.

I bind this day to me forever,
By power of faith, Christ's incarnation,
His baptism in the Jordan River,
His cross of death for my salvation,
His bursting from the spicèd tomb,
His riding up the heavenly way,
His coming at the day of doom,
I bind unto myself today.

I bind unto myself today
The virtues of the starlit heaven,
The glorious sun's life-giving ray,
The whiteness of the moon at even,
The flashing of the lightning free,
The whirling wind's tempestuous shocks,
The stable earth, the deep salt sea,
Around the old eternal rock.

I bind unto myself today
The power of God to hold and lead,
His eye to watch, his might to stay,
His ear to hearken to my need,
The wisdom of my God to teach,
His hand to guide, his shield to ward,
The Word of God to give me speech,
His heavenly host to be my guard.

I bind unto myself the name,
The strong name of the Trinity.
By invocation of the same,
The Three in One and One in Three,
Of whom all nature has creation,
Eternal Father, Spirit, Word,
Praise to the Lord of my salvation,
Salvation is of Christ the Lord.

## God Himself Is with Us

Gerhardt Tersteegen (1729) 6.6.8.6.6.8.3.3.6.6
Trans. *The Hymnal 1940*
St. 2, Henry Sloane Coffin (1910)

God himself is with us;
Let us all adore him,
And with awe appear before him.
God is here within us;
Soul, in silence fear him,
Humbly, fervently draw near him.
Now his own who have known
God, in worship lowly,
Yield their spirits wholly.

Thou pervadest all things:
Let thy radiant beauty
Light mine eyes to see my duty.
As the tender flowers
Eagerly unfold them,
To the sunlight calmly hold them,
So let me quietly
In thy rays imbue me;
Let thy light shine through me.

Stanza 2 used by permission of David D. Coffin.

Come, abide within me;
Let my soul, like Mary,
Be thine earthly sanctuary.
Come, indwelling Spirit,
With transfigured splendor;
Love and honor will I render.
Where I go here below,
Let me bow before thee,
Know thee, and adore thee.

Gladly we surrender
Earth's deceitful treasures,
Pride of life, and sinful pleasures:
Gladly, Lord, we offer
Thine to be forever,
Soul and life and each endeavor.
Thou alone shalt be known
Lord of all our being,
Life's true way decreeing.

# Holy God, We Praise Your Name

*Te Deum laudamus*                                          7.8.7.8.7.7
Vers. attr. Ignaz Franz (c. 1774)
Trans. Clarence Alphonsus Walworth (c. 1853)

Holy God, we praise your name;
Lord of all, we bow before you;
All on earth your scepter claim,
All in heaven above adore you.
Infinite your vast domain,
Everlasting is your reign.

Hark, the glad celestial hymn
Angel choirs above are raising;
Cherubim and seraphim,
In unceasing chorus praising,
Fill the heavens with sweet accord:
Holy, holy, holy Lord.

All apostles join the strain
As your sacred name they hallow;
Prophets swell the glad refrain,
And the blessed martyrs follow,
And from morn to set of sun,
Through the church the song goes on.

Holy Father, Holy Son,
Holy Spirit: Three we name you,
While in essence only One;
Undivided God we claim you,
And adoring bend the knee
While we own the mystery.

# Open Now Thy Gates of Beauty

Benjamin Schmolck (1732)                                    8.7.8.7.7.7
Trans. Catherine Winkworth (1863)

Open now thy gates of beauty,
Zion, let me enter there,
Where my soul in joyful duty
Waits for God who answers prayer;
O how blessed is this place,
Filled with solace, light, and grace.

Gracious God, I come before thee,
Come thou also down to me;
Where we find thee and adore thee,
There a heaven on earth must be;
To my heart O enter thou,
Let it be thy temple now.

Speak, O Lord, and I will hear thee,
Let thy will be done indeed;
May I undisturbed draw near thee,
While thou dost thy people feed.
Here of life the fountain flows,
Here is balm for all our woes.

## In Thee Is Gladness

Johann Lindemann (1598)
Trans. Catherine Winkworth (1858)

In thee is gladness amid all sadness,
Jesus, sunshine of my heart.
By thee are given the gifts of heaven,
Thou the true Redeemer art.
Our souls thou wakest; our bonds thou breakest.
Who trusts thee surely has built securely
And stands forever: Alleluia!
Our hearts are pining to see thy shining,
Dying or living, to thee are cleaving;
Naught us can sever: Alleluia!

If he is ours, we fear no powers,
Not of earth or sin or death.
He sees and blesses in worst distresses;
He can change them with a breath.
Wherefore the story: tell of his glory
With heart and voices; all heaven rejoices
In him forever: Alleluia!
We shout for gladness, triumph o'er sadness,
Love him and praise him and still shall raise him
Glad hymns forever: Alleluia!

# My God, How Wonderful Thou Art

Frederick William Faber (1849)                              CM

My God, how wonderful thou art,
Thy majesty, how bright;
How beautiful thy mercy-seat,
In depths of burning light!

How wonderful, how beautiful
The sight of thee must be,
Thine endless wisdom, boundless power,
And awesome purity!

O how I fear thee, living God,
With deepest, tenderest fears,
And worship thee with trembling hope
And penitential tears!

Yet I may love thee too, O Lord,
Almighty as thou art,
For thou hast stooped to ask of me
The love of my poor heart.

No earthly father loves like thee;
No mother half so mild
Bears and forbears as thou hast done
With me, thy sinful child.

Father of Jesus, Love divine,
Great King upon thy throne,
What joy to see thee as thou art
And worship thee alone.

# Now Thank We All Our God

Martin Rinkart (1636)                                              6.7.6.7.6.6.6.6
Trans. Catherine Winkworth (1858)

Now thank we all our God
With heart and hands and voices,
Who wondrous things hath done,
In whom this world rejoices;
Who, from our mothers' arms,
Hath blessed us on our way
With countless gifts of love,
And still is ours today.

O may this bounteous God
Through all our life be near us,
With ever joyful hearts
And blessed peace to cheer us;
And keep us in God's grace,
And guide us when perplexed,
And free us from all ills
In this world and the next.

All praise and thanks to God,
Who reigns in highest heaven,
To Father and to Son
And Spirit now be given.
The one eternal God,
Whom heaven and earth adore,
The God who was, and is,
And shall be evermore.

# O That I Had a Thousand Voices

Johann Mentzer (1704)                                         9.8.9.8.8.8
Trans. *The Lutheran Hymnal* (1941)

O that I had a thousand voices
To praise my God with thousand tongues!
My heart, which in the Lord rejoices,
Would then proclaim in grateful songs
To all, wherever I might be,
What great things God has done for me!

O all you powers that God implanted,
Arise, keep silence now no more;
Put forth the strength that God has granted!
Your noblest work is to adore!
O soul and body, join to raise
With heartfelt joy our Maker's praise!

You forest leaves so green and tender
That dance for joy in summer air,
You meadow grasses, bright and slender,
You flowers so fragrant and so fair,
You live to show God's praise alone.
Join me to make God's glory known!

All creatures that have breath and motion,
That throng the earth, the sea, the sky,
Come, share with me my heart's devotion,
Help me to sing God's praises high!
My utmost powers can never quite
Declare the wonders of God's might!

# O Worship the King, All Glorious Above!

Robert Grant (1833)                                    10.10.11.11
                                                       Psalm 104

O worship the King, all glorious above!
O gratefully sing his power and his love!
Our shield and defender, the Ancient of Days,
Pavilioned in splendor, and girded with praise.

O tell of his might! O sing of his grace!
Whose robe is the light, whose canopy space.
His chariots of wrath the deep thunderclouds form,
And dark is his path on the wings of the storm.

The earth, with its store of wonders untold,
Almighty, thy power hath founded of old,
Hath stablished it fast by a changeless decree,
And round it hath cast, like a mantle, the sea.

Thy bountiful care, what tongue can recite?
It breathes in the air; it shines in the light;
It streams from the hills; it descends to the plain,
And sweetly distils in the dew and the rain.

Frail children of dust, and feeble as frail,
In thee do we trust, nor find thee to fail;
Thy mercies, how tender! how firm to the end!
Our maker, defender, redeemer, and friend!

# The God of Abraham Praise

*Yigdal* (14th cent.)                                              6.6.8.4 D
Thomas Olivers (1760)

The God of Abraham praise,
Who reigns enthroned above;
Ancient of everlasting days,
And God of love;
To him uplift your voice,
At whose supreme command
From earth we rise, and seek the joys
At his right hand.

Though nature's strength decay,
And earth and hell withstand,
To Canaan's bound we urge our way
At his command.
The watery deep we pass
With Jesus in our view;
And through the howling wilderness
Our way pursue.

The goodly land we see
With peace and plenty blest;
A land of sacred liberty
And endless rest;
There milk and honey flow,
And oil and wine abound,
And trees of life forever grow,
With mercy crowned.

*(continued)*

There dwells the Lord our King,
The Lord our Righteousness,
Triumphant o'er the world and sin,
The Prince of Peace;
On Zion's sacred height
His kingdom he maintains,
And glorious with his saints in light
Forever reigns.

Before the great Three-One
They all exulting stand,
And tell the wonders he hath done
Through all their land;
The listening spheres attend
And swell the growing fame,
And sing, in songs which never end,
The wondrous Name.

The God who reigns on high
The great archangels sing,
And "Holy, holy, holy!" cry,
"Almighty King!
Who was, and is, the same,
And evermore shall be:
Eternal Father, great I AM,
We worship thee!"

Before the Savior's face
The ransomed nations bow,
O'erwhelmed at his almighty grace,
Forever new;
He shows his prints of love:
They kindle to a flame,
And sound through all the worlds above,
"Worthy the Lamb!"

The whole triumphant host
Give thanks to God on high;
"Hail, Father, Son, and Holy Ghost!"
They ever cry;
Hail, Abraham's God, and mine!
I join the heavenly lays.
All might and majesty are thine,
And endless praise.


## Immortal, Invisible, God Only Wise

Walter Chalmers Smith (1867)                                    11.11.11.11

Immortal, invisible, God only wise,
In light inaccessible hid from our eyes,
Most blessed, most glorious, the Ancient of Days,
Almighty, victorious, thy great name we praise.

Unresting, unhasting, and silent as light,
Nor wanting, nor wasting, thou rulest in might;
Thy justice like mountains high soaring above
Thy clouds, which are fountains of goodness and love.

To all, life thou givest, to both great and small;
In all life thou livest, the true life of all;
We blossom and flourish like leaves on the tree,
Then wither and perish; but naught changeth thee.

All praise we would render; O help us to see
'Tis only the splendor of light hideth thee!
And now let thy glory to our gaze unroll
Through Christ in the story, and Christ in the soul.

## Sing Praise to God, Who Reigns Above

Johann Jacob Schütz (1675)                                8.7.8.7.8.8.7
Trans. Frances Elizabeth Cox (1864)

Sing praise to God, who reigns above,
The God of all creation,
The God of power, the God of love,
The God of our salvation;
With healing balm my soul is filled,
And every faithless murmur stilled:
To God all praise and glory!

What God's almighty power hath made,
God's gracious mercy keepeth;
By morning glow or evening shade
God's watchful eye ne'er sleepeth;
Within the kingdom of God's might,
Lo! all is just and all is right:
To God all praise and glory!

The Lord is never far away,
But through all grief distressing,
An ever present help and stay,
Our peace, and joy, and blessing;
As with a mother's tender hand,
God gently leads the chosen band:
To God all praise and glory!

Thus all my gladsome way along,
I sing aloud thy praises
That all may hear the grateful song
My voice unwearied raises.
Be joyful in the Lord, my heart,
Both soul and body take your part:
To God all praise and glory!

# Praise, My Soul, the King of Heaven

Henry Francis Lyte (1834)                                8.7.8.7.8.7
                                                          Psalm 103

Praise, my soul, the King of heaven;
To his feet thy tribute bring;
Ransomed, healed, restored, forgiven,
Evermore his praises sing:
Alleluia! Alleluia!
Praise the everlasting King.

Praise Him for his grace and favor
To his people in distress;
Praise him still the same as ever,
Slow to chide, and swift to bless:
Alleluia! Alleluia!
Glorious in his faithfulness.

Fatherlike he tends and spares us;
Well our feeble frame he knows;
In his hands he gently bears us,
Rescues us from all our foes.
Alleluia! Alleluia!
Widely yet his mercy flows.

Angels, help us to adore him:
Ye behold him face to face;
Sun and moon, bow down before him,
Dwellers all in time and space.
Alleluia! Alleluia!
Praise with us the God of grace.

# Praise to the Lord, the Almighty

Joachim Neander (1680)                                 14.14.4.7.8
Trans. Catherine Winkworth (1863)                      Psalms 103; 150

Praise to the Lord, the Almighty, the King of creation;
O my soul, praise him, for he is thy health and salvation:
All ye who hear,
Now to his temple draw near;
Joining in glad adoration.

Praise to the Lord, who o'er all things so wondrously
   reigneth,
Shelters thee under his wings, yea, so gently sustaineth:
Hast thou not seen?
All that is needful hath been
Granted in what he ordaineth.

Praise to the Lord, who doth prosper thy work and
   defend thee;
Surely his goodness and mercy here daily attend thee.
Ponder anew
What the Almighty can do,
If with his love he befriend thee!

*(continued)*

Praise to the Lord, O let all that is in me adore him;
All that hath life and breath, come now with praises
　before him!
Let the Amen
Sound from his people again;
Gladly forever we adore him.


# When in Our Music God Is Glorified

Fred Pratt Green (1971)　　　　　　　　　　　　10.10.10 Alleluias

When in our music God is glorified,
And adoration leaves no room for pride,
It is as though the whole creation cried
Alleluia!

How often, making music, we have found
A new dimension in the world of sound,
As worship moved us to a more profound
Alleluia!

So has the church in liturgy and song,
In faith and love, through centuries of wrong,
Borne witness to the truth in every tongue,
Alleluia!

And did not Jesus sing a psalm that night
When utmost evil strove against the light?
Then let us sing, for whom he won the fight:
Alleluia!

Let every instrument be tuned for praise!
Let all rejoice who have a voice to raise!
And may God give us faith to sing always
Alleluia!

# All Who Inhabit Planet Earth

Francis of Assisi (c. 1225)                        8.8.4.4.8.8 Alleluias
Trans. Ross Mackenzie (1992)

All who inhabit planet earth—
Join us in praising God with mirth:
Alleluia, Alleluia!
Shine, Brother Sun, with splendid ray,
And, Sister Moon, turn night to day:
Alleluia, Alleluia, Alleluia, Alleluia, Alleluia!

Come, Brother Wind, and bring your friends—
Calm Weather, Breeze, and wild West Winds—
Join our praises, Alleluia!
Shower down upon us, streams of rain,
Great ocean, and the bounding main:
Sister Water, bring your laughter,
Alleluia, Alleluia, Alleluia!

Lighten our darkness, Brother Fire,
Lift up our spirits, ever higher:
Alleluia, Alleluia!
Sustain and feed us, Mother Earth,
Make all our music sing with mirth,
Alleluia, Alleluia, Tra-la-la-la, Tra-la-la-la, Alleluia!

Come, Sister Death, and add your voice;
For you can teach us to rejoice:
Alleluia, Alleluia!
You do no harm to those who love;
You hold the keys of heaven above:
You are our guide to the Lord's side,
Alleluia, Alleluia, Alleluia!

All who inhabit planet earth—
Join us in praising God with mirth:
Alleluia, Alleluia!
Sing praise to Christ, the Virgin's Son,
In whom our new life has begun:
Alleluia, Alleluia, Alleluia, Alleluia, Alleluia!

# God of the Sparrow

Jaroslav J. Vajda (1983)                                        5.4.6.7.7

God of the sparrow
God of the whale
God of the swirling stars
How does the creature say Awe
How does the creature say Praise

God of the earthquake
God of the storm
God of the trumpet blast
How does the creature cry Woe
How does the creature cry Save

God of the rainbow
God of the cross
God of the empty grave
How does the creature say Grace
How does the creature say Thanks

God of the hungry
God of the sick
God of the prodigal
How does the creature say Care
How does the creature say Life

God of the neighbor
God of the foe
God of the pruning hook
How does the creature say Love
How does the creature say Peace

God of the ages
God of the hand
God of the loving heart
How do your children say Joy
How do your children say Home

# How Marvelous God's Greatness

Valdimar Briem (1886)                                           7.6.7.6 D
Trans. Charles V. Pilcher (1913)

How marvelous God's greatness,
How glorious his might!
To this the world bears witness
In wonders day and night.
In form of flower and snowflake,
In morn's resplendent birth,
In afterglow at even,
In sky and sea and earth.

Each tiny floweret whispers
The great Life-giver's name;
The mighty mountain masses
His majesty proclaim;
The hollow vales are hymning
God's shelter for his own;
The snow-capped peaks are pointing
To God's almighty throne.

The ocean's vast abysses
In one grand psalm record
The deep mysterious counsels
And mercies of the Lord;
The icy waves of winter
Are thundering on the strand;
And grief's chill stream is guided
By God's all-gracious hand.

The starry hosts are singing
Through all the light-strewn sky
Of God's majestic temple
And palace courts on high;
When in these outer chambers
Such glory gilds the night,
Oh, what transcendent brightness
Is God's eternal light!

# God, Who Stretched the Spangled Heavens

Catherine Arnott Cameron (1967)                                            8.7.8.7 D

God, who stretched the spangled heavens
Infinite in time and place,
Flung the suns in burning radiance
Through the silent fields of space:
We, your children in your likeness,
Share inventive powers with you;
Great Creator, still creating,
Show us what we yet may do.

We have ventured worlds undreamed of
Since the childhood of our race;
Known the ecstasy of winging
Through untraveled realms of space;
Probed the secrets of the atom,
Yielding unimagined power,
Facing us with life's destruction
Or our most triumphant hour.

As each far horizon beckons,
May it challenge us anew:
Children of creative purpose,
Serving others, honoring you.
May our dreams prove rich with promise,
Each endeavor well begun;
Great Creator, give us guidance
Till our goals and yours are one.

## Joyful, Joyful, We Adore Thee

Henry van Dyke (1907)                                    8.7.8.7 D

Joyful, joyful, we adore thee,
God of glory, Lord of love;
Hearts unfold like flowers before thee,
Opening to the sun above.
Melt the clouds of sin and sadness;
Drive the gloom of doubt away;
Giver of immortal gladness,
Fill us with the light of day.

All thy works with joy surround thee,
Earth and heaven reflect thy rays,
Stars and angels sing around thee,
Center of unbroken praise.
Field and forest, vale and mountain,
Flowery meadow, flashing sea,
Chanting bird and flowing fountain,
Call us to rejoice in thee.

Mortals, join the happy chorus
Which the morning stars began;
Love divine is reigning o'er us,
Joining all in heaven's plan.
Ever singing, march we onward,
Victors in the midst of strife,
Joyful music leads us sunward
In the triumph song of life.

# Come, Ye Thankful People, Come

Henry Alford (1844)                                          7.7.7.7 D
Matthew 15:24–30

Come, ye thankful people, come,
Raise the song of harvest home:
All is safely gathered in,
Ere the winter storms begin;
God, our Maker, doth provide
For our wants to be supplied:
Come to God's own temple, come,
Raise the song of harvest home.

All the world is God's own field,
Fruit unto God's praise to yield;
Wheat and tares together sown,
Unto joy or sorrow grown;
First the blade, and then the ear,
Then the full corn shall appear:
Lord of harvest, grant that we
Wholesome grain and pure may be.

For the Lord our God shall come,
And shall take the harvest home;
From each field shall in that day
All offenses purge away;
Give the angels charge at last
In the fire the tares to cast,
But the fruitful ears to store
In God's garner evermore.

Even so, Lord, quickly come
To thy final harvest home;
Gather thou thy people in,
Free from sorrow, free from sin;
There forever purified,
In thy presence to abide:
Come, with all thine angels, come,
Raise the glorious harvest home.

# I Sing the Mighty Power of God

Isaac Watts (1715)                                                    CMD

I sing the mighty power of God
That made the mountains rise;
That spread the flowing seas abroad
And built the lofty skies.
I sing the wisdom that ordained
The sun to rule the day;
The moon shines full at God's command,
And all the stars obey.

I sing the goodness of the Lord
That filled the earth with food;
God formed the creatures with a word
And then pronounced them good.
Lord, how thy wonders are displayed,
Where'er I turn my eyes;
If I survey the ground I tread,
Or gaze upon the skies!

There's not a plant or flower below
But makes thy glories known;
And clouds arise, and tempests blow,
By order from thy throne;
While all that borrows life from thee
Is ever in thy care,
And everywhere that we can be,
Thou, God, art present there.

# Thank You, God, for Water, Soil, and Air

Brian Wren (1973)                                                    9.10.9.10

Thank you, God, for water, soil, and air,
Large gifts supporting everything that lives.
Forgive our spoiling and abuse of them.
Help us renew the face of the earth.

Thank you, God, for minerals and ores,
The basis of all building, wealth, and speed.
Forgive our reckless plundering and waste.
Help us renew the face of the earth.

Thank you, God, for priceless energy,
Stored in each atom, gathered from the sun.
Forgive our greed and carelessness of power.
Help us renew the face of the earth.

Thank you, God, for weaving nature's life
Into a seamless robe, a fragile whole.
Forgive our haste that tampers unaware.
Help us renew the face of the earth.

Thank you, God, for making planet earth
A home for us and ages yet unborn.
Help us to share, consider, save, and store.
Come and renew the face of the earth.

## For the Fruit of All Creation

Fred Pratt Green (1970)                                      8.4.8.4.8.8.8.4

For the fruit of all creation,
Thanks be to God.
For the gifts to every nation,
Thanks be to God.
For the plowing, sowing, reaping,
Silent growth while we are sleeping,
Future needs in earth's safekeeping,
Thanks be to God.

In the just reward of labor,
God's will be done.
In the help we give our neighbor,
God's will be done.
In our worldwide task of caring
For the hungry and despairing,
In the harvests we are sharing,
God's will be done.

For the harvests of the Spirit,
Thanks be to God.
For the good we all inherit,
Thanks be to God.
For the wonders that astound us,
For the truths that still confound us,
Most of all that love has found us,
Thanks be to God.

# For the Beauty of the Earth

Folliott Sandford Pierpoint (1864)                                      7.7.7.7.7.7

For the beauty of the earth,
For the glory of the skies,
For the love which from our birth
Over and around us lies:

For the wonder of each hour
Of the day and of the night,
Hill and vale, and tree and flower,
Sun and moon, and stars of light:

For the joy of ear and eye,
For the heart and mind's delight,
For the mystic harmony
Linking sense to sound and sight:

For the joy of human love,
Brother, sister, parent, child,
Friends on earth, and friends above,
For all gentle thoughts and mild:

For thy church that evermore
Lifteth holy hands above,
Offering up on every shore
Her pure sacrifice of love:

Lord of all, to thee we raise
This our hymn of grateful praise.

## By Gracious Powers

Dietrich Bonhoeffer (1944)                                    11.10.11.10
Trans. Fred Pratt Green (1972)

By gracious powers so wonderfully sheltered,
And confidently waiting, come what may,
We know that God is with us night and morning
And never fails to greet us each new day.

Yet is this heart by its old foe tormented,
Still evil days bring burdens hard to bear;
O give our frightened souls the sure salvation
For which, O Lord, you taught us to prepare.

And when this cup you give is filled to brimming
With bitter suffering, hard to understand,
We take it thankfully and without trembling,
Out of so good and so beloved a hand.

Yet when again in this same world you give us
The joy we had, the brightness of your sun,
We shall remember all the days we lived through,
And our whole life shall then be yours alone.

# The Care the Eagle Gives Her Young

R. Deane Postlethwaite (1980)

CM
Deuteronomy 32:11

The care the eagle gives her young,
Safe in her lofty nest,
Is like the tender love of God
For us made manifest.

As when the time to venture comes,
She stirs them out to flight,
So we are pressed to boldly try,
To strive for daring height.

And if we flutter helplessly,
As fledgling eagles fall,
Beneath us lift God's mighty wings
To bear us, one and all.

## Commit Thou All Thy Griefs

Paul Gerhardt (1676)                                             SM
Trans. John Wesley (1737)

Commit thou all thy griefs
And ways into his hands,
To his sure truth and tender care
Who earth and heaven commands.

Who points the clouds their course,
Whom winds and seas obey:
He shall direct thy wandering feet,
He shall prepare thy way.

Thou on the Lord rely,
So safe shalt thou go on;
Fix on his work thy steadfast eye,
So shall thy work be done.

No profit canst thou gain
From self-consuming care;
To him commend thy cause; his ear
Attends the softest prayer.

Give to the winds thy fears;
Hope, and be undismayed;
God hears thy sighs and counts thy tears;
God shall lift up thy head.

Through waves and clouds and storms
He gently clears thy way;
Wait thou his time, so shall this night
Soon end in joyous day.

Leave to his sovereign sway
To choose and to command;
So shalt thou, wondering, own his way,
How wise, how strong his hand.

Far, far above thy thought
His counsel shall appear,
When fully he the work hath wrought
That caused thy needless fear.

Thy everlasting truth,
Father, thy ceaseless love,
Sees all thy children's wants, and knows
What best for each will prove.

Thou everywhere hast sway,
And all things serve thy might;
Thy every act pure blessing is,
Thy path unsullied light.

Thou seest our weakness, Lord;
Our hearts are known to thee;
O lift thou up the sinking hand,
Confirm the feeble knee.

Let us in life, in death,
Thy steadfast will declare,
And publish with our latest breath
Thy love and guardian care.

## God Moves in a Mysterious Way
William Cowper (1774)                                              CM

God moves in a mysterious way
His wonders to perform;
He plants his footsteps in the sea,
And rides upon the storm.

Deep in unfathomable mines
Of never-failing skill
He treasures up his bright designs,
And works his sovereign will.

Ye fearful saints, fresh courage take;
The clouds ye so much dread
Are big with mercy, and shall break
In blessings on your head.

Judge not the Lord by feeble sense,
But trust him for his grace;
Behind a frowning providence
He hides a smiling face.

His purposes will ripen fast,
Unfolding every hour;
The bud may have a bitter taste,
But sweet will be the flower.

Blind unbelief is sure to err,
And scan his work in vain;
God is his own interpreter,
And he will make it plain.

# Great Is Thy Faithfulness

Thomas Obediah Chisholm (1923)                    11.10.11.10 Refrain
                                                  Lamentations 3:22–23

Great is thy faithfulness, O God my Father,
There is no shadow of turning with thee;
Thou changest not, thy compassions they fail not;
As thou hast been thou forever wilt be.

Summer and winter, and springtime and harvest,
Sun, moon, and stars in their courses above
Join with all nature in manifold witness
To thy great faithfulness, mercy, and love.

Pardon for sin and a peace that endureth,
Thine own dear presence to cheer and to guide;
Strength for today and bright hope for tomorrow,
Blessings all mine, with ten thousand beside!

Great is thy faithfulness!
Morning by morning new mercies I see;
All I have needed thy hand hath provided;
Great is thy faithfulness, Lord, unto me!

# Guide Me, O Thou Great Jehovah

William Williams (1745)  8.7.8.7.8.7
St. 1 trans. Peter Williams (1771)
Sts. 2–3 trans. William Williams (1772)

Guide me, O thou great Jehovah,
Pilgrim through this barren land;
I am weak, but thou art mighty;
Hold me with thy powerful hand;
Bread of heaven, bread of heaven,
Feed me till I want no more.

Open now the crystal fountain,
Whence the healing stream doth flow;
Let the fire and cloudy pillar
Lead me all my journey through;
Strong deliverer, strong deliverer,
Be thou still my strength and shield.

When I tread the verge of Jordan,
Bid my anxious fears subside;
Death of death, and hell's destruction,
Land me safe on Canaan's side;
Songs of praises, songs of praises
I will ever give to thee.

# He Leadeth Me: O Blessed Thought!

Joseph H. Gilmore (1862)                                                    LM

He leadeth me: O blessed thought!
O words with heavenly comfort fraught!
Whate'er I do, where'er I be,
Still 'tis God's hand that leadeth me.

Sometimes mid scenes of deepest gloom,
Sometimes where Eden's bowers bloom,
By waters still, o'er troubled sea,
Still 'tis his hand that leadeth me.

Lord, I would place my hand in thine,
Nor ever murmur nor repine;
Content, whatever lot I see,
Since 'tis my God that leadeth me.

And when my task on earth is done,
When by thy grace the victory's won,
E'en death's cold wave I will not flee,
Since God through Jordan leadeth me.

He leadeth me, he leadeth me,
By his own hand he leadeth me;
His faithful follower I would be,
For by his hand he leadeth me.

# If Thou But Trust in God to Guide Thee

Georg Neumark (1657)                                        9.8.9.8.8.8
Trans. Catherine Winkworth (1863)

If thou but trust in God to guide thee,
And hope in him through all thy ways,
He'll give thee strength, whate'er betide thee,
And bear thee through the evil days;
Who trusts in God's unchanging love
Builds on the rock that nought can move.

What can these anxious cares avail thee,
These never-ceasing moans and sighs?
What can it help, if thou bewail thee,
O'er each dark moment as it flies?
Our cross and trials do but press
The heavier for our bitterness.

Only be still, and wait his leisure
In cheerful hope, with heart content
To take whate'er thy Father's pleasure
And all-discerning love have sent;
Nor doubt our inmost wants are known
To him who chose us for his own.

Sing, pray, and keep his ways unswerving;
In all thy labor faithful be,
And trust his word, though undeserving,
Thou yet shalt find it true for thee:
God never will forsake in need
The soul that trusts in him indeed.

# My Shepherd Will Supply My Need

Isaac Watts (1719)                                              CMD
                                                              Psalm 23

My Shepherd will supply my need;
Jehovah is his name:
In pastures fresh he makes me feed,
Beside the living stream.
He brings my wandering spirit back,
When I forsake his ways;
And leads me, for his mercy's sake,
In paths of truth and grace.

When I walk through the shades of death
Your presence is my stay;
One word of your supporting breath
Drives all my fears away.
Your hand, in sight of all my foes,
Does still my table spread;
My cup with blessings overflows,
Your oil anoints my head.

The sure provisions of my God
Attend me all my days;
O may your house be my abode,
And all my work be praise.
There would I find a settled rest,
While others go and come;
No more a stranger, or a guest,
But like a child at home.

# Come, Thou Long-Expected Jesus

Charles Wesley (1744)                                              8.7.8.7

Come, thou long-expected Jesus,
Born to set thy people free;
From our fears and sins release us;
Let us find our rest in thee.

Israel's strength and consolation,
Hope of all the earth thou art;
Dear desire of every nation,
Joy of every longing heart.

Born thy people to deliver,
Born a child and yet a King,
Born to reign in us forever,
Now thy gracious kingdom bring.

By thine own eternal Spirit
Rule in all our hearts alone;
By thine all-sufficient merit
Raise us to thy glorious throne.

# O Lord, How Shall I Meet You

Paul Gerhardt (1653)                                                   7.6.7.6 D
Trans. Catherine Winkworth (1863)
  and others

O Lord, how shall I meet you,
How welcome you aright?
Your people long to greet you,
My hope, my heart's delight!
O kindle, Lord most holy,
A lamp within my breast,
To do in spirit lowly
All that may please you best.

Love caused your incarnation,
Love brought you down to me;
Your thirst for my salvation
Procured my liberty.
O love beyond all telling,
That led you to embrace
In love all loves excelling
Our lost and fallen race.

A glorious crown you give me,
A treasure safe on high,
That will not fail nor leave me
As earthly riches fly.
My heart shall bloom forever
For you with praises new,
And from your name shall never
Withhold the honor due.

# Wake, Awake, for Night Is Flying

Philipp Nicolai (1599)                                        Matthew 25:1–13
Trans. Catherine Winkworth (1858)

Wake, awake, for night is flying;
The watchmen on the heights are crying:
Awake, Jerusalem, at last!
Midnight hears the welcome voices
And at the thrilling cry rejoices;
Come forth, ye virgins, night is past;
The Bridegroom comes, awake;
Your lamps with gladness take: Alleluia!
And for his marriage feast prepare,
For ye must go and meet him there.

Zion hears the watchmen singing,
And all her heart with joy is springing;
She wakes, she rises from her gloom;
For her Lord comes down all-glorious,
The strong in grace, in truth victorious.
Her Star is risen; her Light is come.
Ah come, thou blessed One,
God's own beloved Son: Alleluia!
We follow till the halls we see
Where thou hast bid us sup with thee.

Now let all the heavens adore thee,
And saints and angels sing before thee,
With harp and cymbal's clearest tone;
Of one pearl each shining portal,
Where we are with the choir immortal
Of angels round thy dazzling throne;

Nor eye hath seen, nor ear
Hath yet attained to hear what there is ours;
But we rejoice and sing to thee
Our hymn of joy eternally.


## Hark, the Glad Sound! The Savior Comes

Philip Doddridge (1735)                                    CM
Isaiah 61:1–2

Hark, the glad sound! The Savior comes,
The Savior promised long:
Let every heart prepare a throne,
And every voice a song.

He comes, the prisoners to release,
In Satan's bondage held:
The gates of brass before him burst,
The iron fetters yield.

He comes, the broken heart to bind,
The bleeding soul to cure:
And with the treasures of his grace
To enrich the humble poor.

Our glad hosannas, Prince of Peace,
Thy welcome shall proclaim;
And heaven's eternal arches ring
With thy beloved Name.

# O Come, O Come, Emmanuel

Latin (12th cent.)                                                    LM Refrain
Trans. composite

O come, O come, Emmanuel,
And ransom captive Israel
That mourns in lonely exile here
Until the Son of God appear.

O come, O Wisdom from on high,
Who ordered all things mightily;
To us the path of knowledge show
And teach us in its ways to go.

O come, O come, great Lord of might,
Who to your tribes on Sinai's height
In ancient times did give the law
In cloud and majesty and awe.

O come, O Branch of Jesse's stem,
Unto your own and rescue them!
From depths of hell your people save,
And give them victory o'er the grave.

O come, O Key of David, come
And open wide our heavenly home.
Make safe for us the heavenward road
And bar the way to death's abode.

O come, O Bright and Morning Star,
And bring us comfort from afar!
Dispel the shadows of the night
And turn our darkness into light.

O come, O King of nations, bind
In one the hearts of all mankind.
Bid all our sad divisions cease
And be yourself our King of Peace.

Rejoice! Rejoice!
Emmanuel shall come to you, O Israel.

## Savior of the Nations, Come

Ambrose of Milan (4th cent.)                                      7.7.7.7
Para. Martin Luther (1524)
Trans. William Morton Reynolds (1850)

Savior of the nations, come,
Virgin's Son, make here your home.
Marvel now, O heaven and earth,
That the Lord chose such a birth.

From the Godhead forth you came,
And return unto the same,
Captive leading death and hell.
High the song of triumph swell!

You, the chosen Holy One,
Have o'er sin the victory won.
Boundless shall your kingdom be;
When shall we its glories see?

Brightly does your manger shine,
Glorious is its light divine.
Let not sin o'ercloud this light;
Ever be our faith thus bright.

## Tell Out, My Soul

*Magnificat*                                         10.10.10.10
Vers. Timothy Dudley-Smith (1961)                    Song of Mary
                                                     Luke 1:46b–55

Tell out, my soul, the greatness of the Lord!
Unnumbered blessings give my spirit voice;
Tender to me the promise of his word;
In God my Savior shall my heart rejoice.

Tell out, my soul, the greatness of his name!
Make known his might, the deeds his arm has done;
His mercy sure, from age to age the same;
His holy name—the Lord, the mighty One.

Tell out, my soul, the greatness of his might!
Powers and dominions lay their glory by.
Proud hearts and stubborn wills are put to flight,
The hungry fed, the humble lifted high.

Tell out, my soul, the glories of his word!
Firm is his promise, and his mercy sure.
Tell out, my soul, the greatness of the Lord
To children's children and forevermore!

# The Angel Gabriel from Heaven Came

Basque carol (1897)                                                10.10.12.10
Trans. Sabine Baring-Gould (1922)                          Luke 1:26–38

The angel Gabriel from heaven came,
His wings as drifted snow, his eyes as flame;
"All hail," said he, "thou lowly maiden Mary,
Most highly favored lady," Gloria!

"For know a blessed Mother thou shalt be,
All generations laud and honor thee,
Thy Son shall be Emmanuel, by seers foretold,
Most highly favored lady," Gloria!

Then gentle Mary meekly bowed her head,
"To me be as it pleaseth God," she said,
"My soul shall laud and magnify his holy name."
Most highly favored lady, Gloria!

Of her, Emmanuel, the Christ, was born
In Bethlehem, all on a Christmas morn,
And Christian folk throughout the world will ever say—
"Most highly favored lady," Gloria!

# Comfort, Comfort Now My People

Johannes Olearius (1671) 8.7.8.7.7.7.8.8
Trans. Catherine Winkworth (1863) Isaiah 40:1–5

Comfort, comfort now my people,
Tell of peace, thus says our God;
Comfort those who sit in darkness
Bowed beneath oppression's load.
Speak you to Jerusalem
Of the peace that waits for them;
Tell them that their sins I cover,
And their warfare now is over.

For the herald's voice is calling
In the desert far and near,
Bidding us to make repentance
Since the kingdom now is here.
O that warning cry obey!
Now prepare for God a way;
Let the valley rise in meeting
And the hills bow down in greeting.

Make you straight what long was crooked,
Make the rougher places plain;
Let your hearts be true and humble,
As befits God's holy reign.
For the glory of the Lord
Now o'er earth is shed abroad;
And all flesh shall see the token
That God's word is never broken.

## Praised Be the God of Israel

*Benedictus*                                    8.7.8.7.8.8.7.8.8.7
Vers. Bert Polman (1986)                         Song of Zechariah
                                                    Luke 1:68–79

Praised be the God of Israel,
Who has redeemed his people;
Through David's house God will excel
And triumph over evil.
As told by prophets long ago,
He frees us from the hateful foe,
Shows mercy to our parents.
God's covenant oath will persevere,
That we may serve him without fear
Each day in true obedience.

My child, you will prepare God's way
As prophet of the Most High,
Announce to people that the day
Of saving knowledge is nigh.
In tender mercy God begins
To save his people from their sins,
From death and desolation.
The light will make the darkness cease
And guide our feet in ways of peace;
The Lord brings us salvation.

## Angels, from the Realms of Glory

Sts. 1–3, James Montgomery (1816)  8.7.8.7.8.7
St. 4, *Salisbury Hymn Book* (1857)

Angels, from the realms of glory,
Wing your flight o'er all the earth;
Ye who sang creation's story
Now proclaim Messiah's birth:

Shepherds, in the fields abiding,
Watching o'er your flocks by night,
God with us is now residing,
Yonder shines the infant light:

Sages, leave your contemplations,
Brighter visions beam afar;
Seek the great desire of nations;
Ye have seen his natal star:

All creation, join in praising
God the Father, Spirit, Son,
Evermore your voices raising
To the eternal Three in One:

Come and worship, come and worship,
Worship Christ, the newborn King!

# O Come, All Ye Faithful

John Francis Wade (c. 1743)
Trans. Frederick Oakeley (1841)
   and others

O come, all ye faithful,
Joyful and triumphant,
O come ye, O come ye to Bethlehem;
Come, and behold him,
Born the King of angels.

God from God,
Light from Light eternal,
Lo! he abhors not the Virgin's womb;
Only begotten
Son of the Father.

Sing, choirs of angels,
Sing in exultation,
Sing, all ye citizens of heaven above;
Glory to God,
Glory in the highest.

See how the shepherds,
Summoned to his cradle,
Leaving their flocks, draw nigh to gaze;
We too will thither
Bend our joyful footsteps.

Child, for us sinners
Poor and in the manger,
We would embrace thee, with love and awe;
Who would not love thee,
Loving us so dearly?

Yea, Lord, we greet thee,
Born this happy morning;
Jesus, to thee be glory given;
Word of the Father,
Now in flesh appearing.

O come, let us adore him,
Christ, the Lord.

# Good Christian Friends, Rejoice

Medieval Latin and German                              6.6.7.7.7.8.5
  (before 1366)
Trans. and para. John Mason Neale (1835)

Good Christian friends, rejoice
With heart, and soul, and voice;
Give ye heed to what we say:
Jesus Christ is born today;
Ox and ass before him bow,
And he is in the manger now.
Christ is born today!

Good Christian friends, rejoice
With heart, and soul, and voice;
Now ye hear of endless bliss:
Jesus Christ was born for this!
He hath opened heaven's door,
And we are blest forevermore.
Christ was born for this!

Good Christian friends, rejoice
With heart, and soul, and voice;
Now ye need not fear the grave:
Jesus Christ was born to save!
Calls you one and calls you all
To gain the everlasting hall.
Christ was born to save!

# From Heaven Above

Martin Luther (1535)                                    LM
Trans. composite

From heaven above to earth I come
To bring good news to everyone!
Glad tidings of great joy I bring
To all the world, and gladly sing:

To you this night is born a child
Of Mary, chosen virgin mild;
This newborn child of lowly birth
Shall be the joy of all the earth.

This is the Christ, God's Son most high,
Who hears your sad and bitter cry;
He will himself your Savior be
And from all sin will set you free.

The blessing which the Father planned
The Son holds in his infant hand,
That in his kingdom, bright and fair,
You may with us his glory share.

These are the signs which you will see
To let you know that it is he:
In manger-bed, in swaddling clothes
The Child who all the earth upholds.

(*continued*)

How glad we'll be to find it so!
Then with the shepherds let us go
To see what God for us has done
In sending us his own dear Son.

Look, look, dear friends, look over there!
What lies within that manger bare?
Who is that lovely little One?
The baby Jesus, God's dear Son.

Welcome to earth, O noble Guest,
Through whom this sinful world is blest!
You turned not from our needs away!
How can our thanks such love repay?

O Lord, you have created all!
How did you come to be so small,
To sweetly sleep in manger-bed
Where lowing cattle lately fed?

Were earth a thousand times as fair
And set with gold and jewels rare,
Still such a cradle would not do
To rock a prince so great as you.

For velvets soft and silken stuff
You have but hay and straw so rough
On which as king so rich and great
To be enthroned in humble state.

O dearest Jesus, holy Child,
Prepare a bed, soft, undefiled,
A holy shrine, within my heart,
That you and I need never part.

My heart for very joy now leaps;
My voice no longer silence keeps,
I too must join the angel throng
To sing with joy his cradle song:

"Glory to God in highest heaven,
Who unto us his Son has given."
With angels sing in pious mirth:
A glad new year to all the earth!

# Hark! The Herald Angels Sing

Charles Wesley (1739)                                    7.7.7.7 D Refrain

Hark! The herald angels sing,
"Glory to the newborn King.
Peace on earth, and mercy mild,
God and sinners reconciled!"
Joyful, all ye nations, rise,
Join the triumph of the skies;
With the angelic host proclaim,
"Christ is born in Bethlehem!"

Christ, by highest heaven adored,
Christ, the everlasting Lord!
Late in time behold him come,
Offspring of the virgin's womb.
Veiled in flesh the Godhead see;
Hail the incarnate Deity,
Pleased in flesh with us to dwell,
Jesus, our Emmanuel.

Hail the heaven-born Prince of Peace!
Hail the sun of righteousness!
Light and life to all he brings,
Risen with healing in his wings.
Mild he lays his glory by,
Born that we no more may die,
Born to raise us from the earth,
Born to give us second birth.

Hark! The herald angels sing,
"Glory to the newborn King!"

# In Peace and Joy I Now Depart

*Nunc dimittis*                                                    8.5.8.4.7.7
Vers. Martin Luther (1524)                              Song of Simeon
Trans. F. Samuel Janzow (1969)                      Luke 2:29–32

In peace and joy I now depart
Since God so wills it.
Serene and confident my heart;
Stillness fills it.
For God promised death would be
No more than quiet slumber.

This is what you have done for me,
My faithful Savior.
In you, Lord, I was made to see
All God's favor.
I now know you as my life,
My help when I am dying.

It was God's love that sent you forth
For our salvation,
Inviting to yourself the earth,
Every nation,
By your wholesome healing Word
Resounding round our planet.

(*continued*)

You are the health and saving light
Of lands in darkness;
You feed and lighten those in night
With your kindness.
All God's people find in you
Their treasure, joy and glory.

# Of the Father's Love Begotten

Marcus Aurelius Clemens Prudentius      8.7.8.7.8.7.7
  (early 5th cent.)
Sts. 1–4 trans. John Mason Neale (1854)
St. 5, Henry Williams Baker (1859)

Of the Father's love begotten,
Ere the worlds began to be,
He is Alpha and Omega,
He the source, the ending he,
Of the things that are, that have been,
And that future years shall see,
Evermore and evermore!

O that birth for ever blessèd,
When the Virgin, full of grace,
By the Holy Ghost conceiving,
Bare the Savior of our race;
And the Babe, the world's Redeemer,
First revealed his sacred face,
Evermore and evermore!

This is he whom seers in old time
Chanted of with one accord;
Whom the voices of the prophets
Promised in their faithful word;
Now he shines, the long-expected;
Let creation praise its Lord;
Evermore and evermore!

O ye heights of heaven adore him;
Angel hosts, his praises sing;
Powers, dominions, bow before him,
And extol our God and King;
Let no tongue on earth be silent,
Every voice in concert ring,
Evermore and evermore!

Christ, to thee with God the Father,
And, O Holy Ghost, to thee,
Hymn and chant and high thanksgiving,
And unwearied praises be:
Honor, glory, and dominion,
And eternal victory,
Evermore and evermore!

# Once in Royal David's City

Sts. 1–2, 4–6, Cecil Frances Alexander (1848)                8.7.8.7.7.7
St. 3, James Waring McCrady (1982)

Once in royal David's city
Stood a lowly cattle shed,
Where a mother laid her baby
In a manger for his bed:
Mary was that mother mild,
Jesus Christ her little Child.

He came down to earth from heaven,
Who is God and Lord of all,
And his shelter was a stable,
And his cradle was a stall;
With the poor, the scorned, the lowly,
Lives on earth our Savior holy.

We, like Mary, rest confounded
That a stable should display
Heaven's Word, the world's Creator,
Cradled there on Christmas Day,
Yet this Child, our Lord and brother,
Brought us love for one another.

For he is our lifelong pattern;
Daily, when on earth he grew,
He was tempted, scorned, rejected,
Tears and smiles like us he knew.
Thus he feels for all our sadness,
And he shares in all our gladness.

And our eyes at last shall see Him
Through his own redeeming love;
For that Child who seemed so helpless
Is our Lord in heaven above;
And he leads his children on—
To the place where he is gone.

Not in that poor lowly stable
With the oxen standing by
We shall see him, but in heaven,
Set at God's right hand on high:
There his children gather round
Bright like stars, with glory crowned.

# All My Heart This Night Rejoices

Paul Gerhardt (1653)                                          8.3.3.6 D
Trans. Catherine Winkworth (1858)

All my heart this night rejoices,
As I hear,
Far and near,
Sweetest angel voices:
"Christ is born," their choirs are singing,
Till the air,
Everywhere,
Now with joy is ringing.

Hark! A voice from yonder manger,
Soft and sweet,
Does entreat:
"Flee from woe and danger;
Come and see; from all that grieves you
You are freed;
All you need
I will surely give you."

Come, then, let us hasten yonder;
Here let all,
Great and small,
Kneel in awe and wonder;
Love him who with love is yearning;
Hail the star
That from far
Bright with hope is burning!

# What Child Is This

William Chatterton Dix (1871)                    8.7.8.7.6.8.6.7

What child is this, who, laid to rest,
On Mary's lap is sleeping?
Whom angels greet with anthems sweet
While shepherds watch are keeping?
This, this is Christ the King,
Whom shepherds guard and angels sing;
Haste, haste to bring him laud,
The babe, the son of Mary!

Why lies he in such mean estate
Where ox and ass are feeding?
Good Christian, fear; for sinners here
The silent Word is pleading.
Nails, spear shall pierce him through,
The cross be borne for me, for you;
Hail, hail the Word made flesh,
The babe, the son of Mary!

So bring him incense, gold, and myrrh;
Come, peasant, king, to own him.
The king of kings salvation brings;
Let loving hearts enthrone him.
Raise, raise the song on high,
The virgin sings her lullaby;
Joy, joy, for Christ is born,
The babe, the son of Mary!

# O Morning Star, How Fair and Bright

Philipp Nicolai (1599)       8.8.7.8.8.7.4.8.4.8
Trans. Catherine Winkworth (1863)
St. 3, *Lutheran Book of Worship* (1978)

O Morning Star, how fair and bright
Thou beamest forth in truth and light,
O Sovereign meek and lowly!
Thou Root of Jesse, David's Son,
My Lord and Master, thou hast won
My heart to serve thee solely!
Thou art holy,
Fair and glorious, all victorious,
Rich in blessing,
Rule and might o'er all possessing.

Thou heavenly Brightness! Light divine!
O deep within my heart now shine,
And make thee there an altar!
Fill me with joy and strength to be
Thy member, ever joined to thee
In love that cannot falter;
Toward thee longing
Doth possess me; turn and bless me;
Here in sadness
Eye and heart long for thy gladness!

What joy to know, when life is past,
The Lord we love is first and last,
The end and the beginning!
He will one day, O glorious grace,
Transport us to that happy place
Beyond all tears and sinning!
Amen! Amen!
Come, Lord Jesus! Crown of gladness,
We are yearning
For the day of your returning.

# Earth Has Many a Noble City

Marcus Aurelius Clemens Prudentius                    8.7.8.7
  (early 5th cent.)                                   Matt. 2:1–6
Trans. *Hymns Ancient and Modern* (1861)

Earth has many a noble city;
Bethlehem, thou dost all excel:
Out of thee the Lord from heaven
Came to rule his Israel.

Fairer than the sun at morning
Was the star that told his birth,
To the world its God announcing
Seen in fleshly form on earth.

Eastern sages at his cradle
Make oblations rich and rare;
See them give, in deep devotion,
Gold and frankincense and myrrh.

Sacred gifts of mystic meaning:
Incense doth their God disclose,
Gold the King of kings proclaimeth,
Myrrh his sepulcher foreshows.

Jesus, whom the Gentiles worshiped
At thy glad epiphany,
Unto thee, with God the Father
And the Spirit, glory be.

## The Only Son from Heaven

Elizabeth Cruciger (1524)                                7.6.7.6.7.7.6
Trans. Arthur Tozer Russell (1851)

The only Son from heaven,
Foretold by ancient seers,
By God the Father given,
In human form appears.
No sphere his light confining,
No star so brightly shining
As he, our Morning Star.

Oh, time of God appointed,
Oh, bright and holy morn!
He comes, the King anointed,
The Christ, the virgin-born,
Grim death to vanquish for us,
To open heaven before us
And bring us life again.

Awaken, Lord, our spirit
To know and love you more,
In faith to stand unshaken,
In spirit to adore,
That we, through this world moving,
Each glimpse of heaven proving,
May reap its fullness there.

(*continued*)

O Father, here before you
With God the Holy Ghost,
And Jesus, we adore you,
O pride of angel host;
Before you mortals lowly
Cry, "Holy, holy, holy,
O blessed Trinity!"


## Hail to the Lord's Anointed

James Montgomery (1821)                              7.6.7.6 D
                                                     Psalm 72

Hail to the Lord's Anointed,
Great David's greater Son!
Hail, in the time appointed,
His reign on earth begun!
He comes to break oppression,
To set the captive free;
To take away transgression,
And rule in equity.

He comes with succor speedy
To those who suffer wrong,
To help the poor and needy,
And bid the weak be strong;
To give them songs for sighing,
Their darkness turn to light,
Whose souls, condemned and dying,
Were precious in his sight.

He shall come down like showers
Upon the fruitful earth,
And love, joy, hope, like flowers,
Spring in his path to birth;
Before him on the mountains
Shall peace, the herald, go;
And righteousness in fountains
From hill to valley flow.

Kings shall bow down before him,
And gold and incense bring;
All nations shall adore him,
His praise all people sing;
To him shall prayer unceasing
And daily vows ascend;
His kingdom still increasing,
A kingdom without end.

O'er every foe victorious,
He on his throne shall rest;
From age to age more glorious,
All-blessing and all-blest:
The tide of time shall never
His covenant remove;
His name shall stand for ever,
His changeless name of Love.

# I Heard the Voice of Jesus Say

Horatius Bonar (1846)                              CMD
Matt. 11:28–30; John 4:13–14;
John 8:12

I heard the voice of Jesus say,
"Come unto me and rest;
Lay down, thou weary one, lay down
Thy head upon my breast."
I came to Jesus as I was,
Weary, and worn, and sad;
I found in him a resting place,
And he has made me glad.

I heard the voice of Jesus say,
"Behold, I freely give
The living water; thirsty one,
Stoop down and drink, and live."
I came to Jesus, and I drank
Of that life-giving stream;
My thirst was quenched, my soul revived,
And now I live in him.

I heard the voice of Jesus say,
"I am this dark world's light;
Look unto me, thy morn shall rise,
And all thy day be bright."
I look to Jesus, and I found
In him my Star, my Sun;
And in that light of life I'll walk
Till traveling days are done.

# Jesu, Jesu, Fill Us with Your Love

Tom Colvin (1969)                                       John 13:1–17

Jesu, Jesu, fill us with your love,
Show us how to serve the neighbors we have from you.

Kneels at the feet of his friends,
Silently washes their feet,
Master who acts as a slave to them.

Neighbors are rich and poor,
Varied in color and race,
Neighbors are near and far away.

These are the ones we should serve,
These are the ones we should love.
All are neighbors to us and you.

Loving puts us on our knees,
Serving as though we are slaves,
This is the way we should live with you.

Kneel at the feet of our friends,
Silently washing their feet,
This is the way we should live with you.

Jesu, Jesu, fill us with your love,
Show us how to serve the neighbors we have from you.

# Jesus Calls Us

Cecil Frances Alexander (1852)                                    8.7.8.7
Matthew 4:18–22

Jesus calls us o'er the tumult
Of our life's wild, restless sea;
Day by day his sweet voice soundeth,
Saying, "Christian, follow me!"

As of old the apostles heard it
By the Galilean lake,
Turned from home and toil and kindred,
Leaving all for Jesus' sake.

Jesus calls us from the worship
Of the vain world's golden store,
From each idol that would keep us,
Saying, "Christian, love me more!"

In our joys and in our sorrows,
Days of toil and hours of ease,
Still he calls, in cares and pleasures,
"Christian, love me more than these!"

Jesus calls us! By thy mercies,
Savior, may we hear thy call,
Give our hearts to thine obedience,
Serve and love thee best of all!

# Lord of All Hopefulness

Jan Struther (1931)                                              10.11.11.12

Lord of all hopefulness, Lord of all joy,
Whose trust, ever childlike, no cares could destroy,
Be there at our waking, and give us, we pray,
Your bliss in our hearts, Lord, at the break of the day.

Lord of all eagerness, Lord of all faith,
Whose strong hands were skilled at the plane and the
  lathe,
Be there at our labors, and give us, we pray,
Your strength in our hearts, Lord, at the noon of the day.

Lord of all kindliness, Lord of all grace,
Your hands swift to welcome, your arms to embrace,
Be there at our homing, and give us, we pray,
Your love in our hearts, Lord, at the eve of the day.

Lord of all gentleness, Lord of all calm,
Whose voice is contentment, whose presence is balm,
Be there at our sleeping, and give us, we pray,
Your peace in our hearts, Lord, at the end of the day.

# O Christ, the Healer

Fred Pratt Green (1969)                                          LM

O Christ, the healer, we have come
To pray for health, to plead for friends.
How can we fail to be restored,
When reached by love that never ends?

From every ailment flesh endures
Our bodies clamor to be freed;
Yet in our hearts we would confess
That wholeness is our deepest need.

How strong, O Lord, are our desires,
How weak our knowledge of ourselves!
Release in us those healing truths
Unconscious pride resists or shelves.

In conflicts that destroy our health
We recognize the world's disease;
Our common life declares our ills:
Is there no cure, O Christ, for these?

Grant that we all, made one in faith,
In your community may find
The wholeness that, enriching us,
Shall reach the whole of humankind.

## Stranger God, You Come to Us

Shirley Erena Murray (1983)                    7.8.8.5.5.7.7

Stranger God, you come to us,
Knock on doors and ask for shelter,
Wash our feet with towel and water,
Teach us how to pray,
Heed what women say.

Stranger with compassion's face,
Here you speak of love and healing,
Shout your anger, cry your feeling,
Show a God that's weak—
Turn the other cheek.

Stranger God, you come to us,
Unexpected, unprotected,
In our body resurrected
Where our hope had died,
Hanging crucified.

Strangest God of all you seem:
Though we mock you, or neglect you,
Never can we so reject you
That you let us go—
Love cannot say "No!"

Stranger God, you come to us,
Stranger God, you come to us.

# Woman in the Night

Brian Wren (1982)  5.5.5.5 Refrain

Woman in the night,
Spent from giving birth,
Guard our precious light:
Peace is on the earth!

Woman in the crowd,
Creeping up behind,
Touching is allowed:
Seek and you will find!

Woman at the well,
Question the Messiah;
Find your friends and tell;
Drink your heart's desire!

Woman at the feast,
Let the righteous stare;
Come and go in peace;
Love him with your hair!

Woman in the house,
Nurtured to be meek,
Leave your second place:
Listen, think, and speak!

Women on the road,
Welcomed and restored,
Travel far and wide;
Witness to the Lord!

Women on the hill,
Stand when men have fled!
Christ needs loving still,
Though your hope is dead.

Women in the dawn,
Care and spices bring;
Earliest to mourn;
Earliest to sing!

Come and join the song,
Women, children, men.
Jesus makes us free
To live again!

# You, Lord, Are Both Lamb and Shepherd

Sylvia G. Dunstan (1984)                                        8.7.8.7.8.7

> You, Lord, are both lamb and shepherd,
> You, Lord, are both prince and slave,
> You, peace-maker and sword-bringer,
> Of the way you took and gave.
> You, the everlasting instant,
> You whom we both scorn and crave.
>
> Clothed in light upon the mountain,
> Stripped of might upon the cross,
> Shining in eternal glory,
> Beggared by a soldier's toss.
> You, the everlasting instant,
> You who are our gift and cost.
>
> You who walk each day beside us,
> Sit in power at God's side,
> You who preach a way that's narrow,
> Have a love that reaches wide.
> You, the everlasting instant,
> You who are our pilgrim guide.
>
> Worthy is our earthly Jesus,
> Worthy is our cosmic Christ,
> Worthy your defeat and victory,
> Worthy still your peace and strife.
> You, the everlasting instant,
> You who are our death and life.

# Your Hand, O Lord, in Days of Old

Edward H. Plumptre (1866)                                                    CMD

Your hand, O Lord, in days of old
Was strong to heal and save;
You triumphed over pain and death,
O'er darkness and the grave.
To you they went, the blind, the mute,
The palsied and the lame,
The leper set apart and shunned,
The sick and those in shame.

And then your touch brought life and health,
Gave speech and strength and sight;
And youth renewed, with health restored,
Claimed you, the Lord of light.
And so, O Lord, be near to bless,
Almighty now as then,
In every street, in every home,
In every troubled friend.

O be our mighty healer still,
O Lord of life and death;
Restore and strengthen, soothe and bless
With your almighty breath.
On hands that work and eyes that see,
Your healing wisdom pour,
That whole and sick and weak and strong
May praise you evermore.

## Forgive Our Sins as We Forgive

Rosamond E. Herklots (1969, 1983)          CM

''Forgive our sins as we forgive,''
You taught us, Lord, to pray,
But you alone can grant us grace
To live the words we say.

How can your pardon reach and bless
The unforgiving heart
That broods on wrongs and will not let
Old bitterness depart?

In blazing light your cross reveals
The truth we dimly knew:
What trivial debts are owed to us,
How great our debt to you!

Lord, cleanse the depths within our souls
And bid resentment cease.
Then, bound to all in bonds of love,
Our lives will spread your peace.

# When Jesus Came to Jordan

Fred Pratt Green (1973)                                        7.6.7.6 D

When Jesus came to Jordan
To be baptized by John,
He did not come for pardon
But as the sinless one.
He came to share repentance
With all who mourn their sins,
To speak the vital sentence
With which good news begins.

He came to share temptation,
Our utmost woe and loss,
For us and our salvation
To die upon the cross.
So when the dove descended
On him, the Son of Man,
The hidden years had ended,
The age of grace began.

Come, Holy Spirit, aid us
To keep the vows we make;
This very day invade us,
And every bondage break.
Come, give our lives direction,
The gift we covet most:
To share the resurrection
That leads to Pentecost.

# Swiftly Pass the Clouds of Glory

Thomas H. Troeger (1985)

8.7.8.7 D
Luke 9:28–36

Swiftly pass the clouds of glory,
Heaven's voice, the dazzling light;
Moses and Elijah vanish;
Christ alone commands the height!
Peter, James, and John fall silent,
Turning from the summit's rise
Downward toward the shadowed valley
Where their Lord has fixed his eyes.

Glimpsed and gone the revelation,
They shall gain and keep its truth,
Not by building on the mountain
Any shrine or sacred booth,
But by following the Savior
Through the valley to the cross
And by testing faith's resilience
Through betrayal, pain, and loss.

Lord, transfigure our perception
With the purest light that shines,
And recast our life's intentions
To the shape of your designs,
Till we seek no other glory
Than what lies past Calvary's hill
And our living and our dying
And our rising by your will.

## Sing of Mary, Pure and Lowly

Roland Ford Palmer (1938)                                              8.7.8.7 D
                                                                       Acts 1:14

Sing of Mary, pure and lowly,
Virgin Mother undefiled.
Sing of God's own Son most holy,
Who became her little child.
Fairest child of fairest Mother,
God the Lord who came to earth,
Word made flesh, our very Brother,
Takes our nature by his birth.

Sing of Jesus, Son of Mary,
In the home at Nazareth.
Toil and labor cannot weary
Love enduring unto death.
Constant was the love he gave her,
Though it drove him from her side,
Forth to preach, and heal, and suffer,
Till on Calvary he died.

Sing of Mary, sing of Jesus,
Holy Mother's holier Son.
From his throne in heaven he sees us,
Thither calls us every one,
Where he welcomes home his Mother
To a place at his right hand,
There his faithful servants gather,
There the crownèd victors stand.

Roland F. Palmer, SSJE. Used by permission of the Anglican Catholic Church of Canada.

Joyful Mother, full of gladness,
In thine arms thy Lord was borne.
Mournful Mother, full of sadness,
All thy heart with pain was torn.
Glorious Mother, now rewarded
With a crown at Jesus' hand,
Age to age thy name recorded
Shall be blest in every land.

Glory be to God the Father;
Glory be to God the Son;
Glory be to God the Spirit;
Glory to the Three in One.
From the heart of blessèd Mary,
From all saints the song ascends,
And the church the strain re-echoes
Unto earth's remotest ends.

## Sing We of the Blessed Mother

George B. Timms (1975)                                    8.7.8.7 D

Sing we of the blessed Mother
Who received the angel's word,
And obedient to the summons
Bore in love the infant Lord;
Sing we of the joys of Mary
At whose breast that child was fed
Who is Son of God eternal
And the everlasting Bread.

Sing we, too, of Mary's sorrows,
Of the sword that pierced her through,
When beneath the cross of Jesus
She his weight of suffering knew,
Looked upon her Son and Savior
Reigning from the awful tree,
Saw the price of our redemption
Paid to set the sinner free.

Sing again the joys of Mary
When she saw the risen Lord,
And in prayer with Christ's apostles,
Waited on his promised word;
From on high the blazing glory
Of the Spirit's presence came,
Heavenly breath of God's own being,
Tokened in the wind and flame.

Sing the greatest joy of Mary
When on earth her work was done,
And the Lord of all creation
Brought her to his heavenly home:
Virgin Mother, Mary blessed,
Raised on high and crowned with grace,
May your Son, the world's Redeemer,
Grant us all to see his face.

## Forty Days and Forty Nights

George Hunt Smyttan (1856)                          7.7.7.7

Forty days and forty nights
You were fasting in the wild;
Forty days and forty nights
Tempted, and yet undefiled.

Shall not we your sorrow share
And from worldly joys abstain,
Fasting with unceasing prayer,
Strong with you to suffer pain?

Then if Satan on us press,
Flesh or spirit to assail,
Victor in the wilderness,
Grant that we not faint nor fail!

So shall we have peace divine:
Holier gladness ours shall be;
Round us, too, shall angels shine,
Such as served you faithfully.

Keep, O keep us, Savior dear,
Ever constant by your side;
That with you we may appear
At the eternal Eastertide.

# O Love, How Deep, How Broad, How High

Attr. Thomas à Kempis (15th cent.)                              LM
Trans. Benjamin Webb
  and John Mason Neale (1851)

O love, how deep, how broad, how high,
How passing thought and fantasy,
That God, the Son of God, should take
Our mortal form for mortals' sake.

For us baptized, for us he bore
His holy fast and hungered sore;
For us temptations sharp he knew,
For us the tempter overthrew.

For us to evil power betrayed,
Scourged, mocked, in purple robe arrayed,
He bore the shameful cross and death,
For us gave up his dying breath.

For us he rose from death again;
For us he went on high to reign;
For us he sent the Spirit here
To guide, to strengthen, and to cheer.

All glory to our Lord and God
For love so deep, so high, so broad:
The Trinity whom we adore
Forever and forevermore.

# A Lamb Goes Uncomplaining Forth

Paul Gerhardt (1648)                                    Isaiah 53:7
Trans. composite

A Lamb goes uncomplaining forth
To save a world of sinners.
He bears the burden all alone,
Dies shorn of all his honors.
He goes to slaughter, weak and faint,
Is led to die without complaint;
His spotless life he offers.
He bears the shame, the stripes, the wrath;
His anguish, mockery, and death
For us he gladly suffers.

This Lamb is Christ, our greatest friend,
The Lamb of God, our Savior,
The One, his only Son, God sent
To win us rebels over.
"Go down, my child," the Father said,
"And free my children from their dread
Of death and condemnation.
The painful stripes are hard to bear,
But by your death they all can share
The joy of your salvation."

He answered from his tender heart
That he would take the burden:
"My Father's will is my command;
I'll do as I am bidden."
Oh, wondrous love! Oh, loving might!
To right what mortals cannot right
God sent his Son from heaven.
What love, O Love, who came to save
By loving even to the grave
Until the stone was riven.

Of death I am no more afraid;
His dying is my living.
He clothes me in his royal robes
That he is always giving.
His love is dress enough for me
To wear through all eternity
Before the highest Father,
Where we shall stand at Jesus' side,
His church, the well-appointed bride,
When all the faithful gather.

# Lord Christ, When First You Came to Earth

Walter Russell Bowie (1928)                                        8.7.8.7.8.8.7

Lord Christ, when first you came to earth,
Upon a cross they bound you,
And mocked your saving kingship then
By thorns with which they crowned you;
And still our wrongs may weave you now
New thorns to pierce that steady brow,
And robe of sorrow round you.

O wondrous love, which found no room
In life, where sin denied you,
And, doomed to death, must bring to doom
The power which crucified you,
Till not a stone was left on stone,
And all a nation's pride, o'erthrown,
Went down to dust beside you.

New advent of the love of Christ,
Shall we again refuse you,
Till in the night of hate and war
We perish as we lose you?
From old unfaith our souls release
To seek the kingdom of your peace,
By which alone we choose you.

O wounded hands of Jesus, build
In us your new creation;
Our pride is dust, our vaunt is stilled,
We wait your revelation.
O Love that triumphs over loss,
We bring our hearts before your cross;
Come, finish your salvation.

## My Song Is Love Unknown

Samuel Crossman (1664)                              6.6.6.6.4.4.4.4

My song is love unknown,
My Savior's love to me,
Love to the loveless shown
That they might lovely be.
O who am I
That for my sake
My Lord should take
Frail flesh, and die?

Christ came from heaven's throne
Salvation to bestow,
But people scorned and none
The longed-for Christ would know.
But O my Friend,
My Friend indeed,
Who at my need
His life did spend!

Sometimes they strew his way,
And his sweet praises sing,
Resounding all the way
Hosannas to their King.
Then "Crucify!"
Is all their breath,
And for his death
They thirst and cry.

They rise, and needs will have
My dear Lord made away;
A murderer they save,
The Prince of life they slay.
Yet steadfast he
To suffering goes,
That he his foes
From thence might free.

Here might I stay and sing,
No story so divine:
Never was love, dear King,
Never was grief like thine.
This is my Friend,
In whose sweet praise
I all my days
Could gladly spend.

# O Lamb of God Most Holy!

*Agnus Dei*                                              7.7.7.7.7.7.7
Vers. Nikolaus Decius (1523)
Trans. Arthur Tozer Russell (1848)

O Lamb of God most holy!
Who on the cross did suffer,
And patient still and lowly,
Yourself to scorn did offer;
Our sins by you were taken,
Or hope had us forsaken:
Have mercy on us, Jesus!

O Lamb of God most holy!
Who on the cross did suffer,
And patient still and lowly,
Yourself to scorn did offer;
Our sins by you were taken,
Or hope had us forsaken:
Have mercy on us, Jesus!

O Lamb of God most holy!
Who on the cross did suffer,
And patient still and lowly,
Yourself to scorn did offer;
Our sins by you were taken,
Or hope had us forsaken:
Your peace be with us, Jesus!

# What Wondrous Love Is This

Anon. U.S.A. (1811) 12.9.12.12.9

What wondrous love is this, O my soul, O my soul,
What wondrous love is this, O my soul!
What wondrous love is this that caused the Lord of bliss
To bear the dreadful curse for my soul, for my soul,
To bear the dreadful curse for my soul!

When I was sinking down, sinking down, sinking down,
When I was sinking down, sinking down,
When I was sinking down beneath God's righteous
    frown,
Christ laid aside his crown for my soul, for my soul,
Christ laid aside his crown for my soul.

To God and to the Lamb I will sing, I will sing,
To God and to the Lamb, I will sing;
To God and to the Lamb who is the great I Am,
While millions join the theme, I will sing, I will sing;
While millions join the theme, I will sing!

And when from death I'm free, I'll sing on, I'll sing on,
And when from death I'm free, I'll sing on;
And when from death I'm free, I'll sing and joyful be,
And through eternity I'll sing on, I'll sing on,
And through eternity I'll sing on!

# Wilt Thou Forgive That Sin

John Donne (c. 1621)                              10.10.10.10.8.4

Wilt thou forgive that sin, where I begun,
Which was my sin though it were done before?
Wilt thou forgive that sin, through which I run,
And do run still, though still I do deplore?
When thou hast done, thou hast not done,
For I have more.

Wilt thou forgive that sin which I have won
Others to sin, and made my sin their door?
Wilt thou forgive that sin which I did shun
A year or two, but wallowed in a score?
When thou hast done, thou hast not done,
For I have more.

I have a sin of fear, that when I've spun
My last thread, I shall perish on the shore;
But swear by thyself, that at my death thy Son
Shall shine, as he shines now and heretofore:
And, having done that, thou hast done:
I fear no more.

# O God, Be Gracious to Me in Your Love

Vers. Ian Pitt-Watson (1973)                    10.10.10.10
                                                Psalm 51:1–12

O God, be gracious to me in your love,
And in your mercy pardon my misdeeds;
Wash me from guilt and cleanse me from my sin,
For well I know the evil I have done.

Against you, Lord, you only, have I sinned,
And what to you is evil have I done;
Take hyssop, sprinkle me and make me clean,
Wash me and make me whiter than the snow.

Fill me with gladness and rejoicing, Lord,
And let my broken frame know joy once more;
Create a clean and contrite heart in me,
Renew my life in faithfulness and love.

Drive me not from your presence, gracious Lord,
Nor keep your Holy Spirit far from me;
Restore my life with your salvation's joy,
And with a willing spirit strengthen me.

# Ride On! Ride On in Majesty!

Henry Hart Milman (1827)　　　　　　　　　　　　　　　　　LM

Ride on! Ride on in majesty!
Hark! all the tribes hosanna cry;
O Savior meek, pursue thy road
With palms and scattered garments strowed.

Ride on! Ride on in majesty!
In lowly pomp ride on to die;
O Christ, thy triumphs now begin
O'er captive death and conquered sin.

Ride on! Ride on in majesty!
The winged squadrons of the sky
Look down with sad and wondering eyes
To see the approaching sacrifice.

Ride on! Ride on in majesty!
In lowly pomp ride on to die;
Bow thy meek head to mortal pain,
Then take, O God, thy power, and reign.

# All Glory, Laud, and Honor

Theodulph of Orleans (c. 820)                              7.6.7.6 D
Trans. John Mason Neale (1851)                            Matt. 21:1–6

All glory, laud, and honor
To thee, Redeemer, King!
To whom the lips of children
Made sweet hosannas ring.

Thou art the King of Israel,
Thou David's royal Son,
Who in the Lord's name comest,
The King and blessed One.

The people of the Hebrews
With palms before thee went;
Our praise and prayers and anthems
Before thee we present.

To thee, before thy passion,
They sang their hymns of praise;
To thee, now high exalted,
Our melody we raise.

Thou didst accept their praises;
Accept the prayers we bring,
Who in all good delightest,
Thou good and gracious King!

All glory, laud, and honor
To thee, Redeemer, King!
To whom the lips of children
Made sweet hosannas ring.

## Go to Dark Gethsemane

James Montgomery (1820, 1825)                    7.7.7.7.7.7

Go to dark Gethsemane,
All who feel the tempter's power;
Your Redeemer's conflict see,
Watch with him one bitter hour;
Turn not from his griefs away,
Learn from Jesus Christ to pray.

Follow to the judgment hall;
View the Lord of life arraigned;
O the wormwood and the gall!
O the pangs his soul sustained!
Shun not suffering, shame, or loss;
Learn from Christ to bear the cross.

Calvary's mournful mountain climb;
There, adoring at his feet,
Mark the miracle of time,
God's own sacrifice complete;
"It is finished!" hear him cry;
Learn from Jesus Christ to die.

Early hasten to the tomb
Where they laid his breathless clay:
All is solitude and gloom.
Who has taken him away?
Christ is risen! he meets our eyes.
Savior, teach us so to rise.

## Sunset to Sunrise Changes Now

Clement of Alexandria (early 3d cent.)                    LM
Trans. Howard Chandler Robbins (1939)

Sunset to sunrise changes now,
For God doth make his world anew:
On the Redeemer's thorn-crowned brow
The wonders of that dawn we view.

E'en though the sun withholds its light,
Lo! a more heavenly lamp shines here,
And from the cross on Calvary's height
Gleams of eternity appear.

Hear in o'erwhelming final strife
The Lord of life hath victory;
And sin is slain, and death brings life,
And sons of earth hold heaven in fee.

# Ah, Holy Jesus

Johann Heermann (1630)                                      11.11.11.5
Trans. Robert Seymour Bridges (1899)

Ah, holy Jesus, how hast thou offended,
That we to judge thee have in hate pretended?
By foes derided, by thine own rejected,
O most afflicted!

Who was the guilty? Who brought this upon thee?
Alas, my treason, Jesus, hath undone thee!
'Twas I, Lord Jesus, I it was denied thee;
I crucified thee.

Lo, the Good Shepherd for the sheep is offered;
The slave hath sinnèd, and the Son hath suffered.
For our atonement, while we nothing heeded,
God interceded.

For me, kind Jesus, was thy incarnation,
Thy mortal sorrow, and thy life's oblation;
Thy death of anguish and thy bitter passion,
For my salvation.

Therefore, kind Jesus, since I cannot pay thee,
I do adore thee, and will ever pray thee,
Think on thy pity and thy love unswerving,
Not my deserving.

# O Sacred Head, Now Wounded

Attr. Bernard of Clairvaux (12th cent.)                    7.6.7.6 D
Paul Gerhardt (1656)
Trans. James Waddell Alexander (1830)

O sacred head, now wounded,
With grief and shame weighed down;
Now scornfully surrounded
With thorns, thine only crown;
O sacred head, what glory,
What bliss till now was thine!
Yet, though despised and gory,
I joy to call thee mine.

What thou, my Lord, hast suffered
Was all for sinners' gain:
Mine, mine was the transgression,
But thine the deadly pain.
Lo, here I fall, my Savior!
'Tis I deserve thy place;
Look on me with thy favor,
Vouchsafe to me thy grace.

What language shall I borrow
To thank thee, dearest friend,
For this thy dying sorrow,
Thy pity without end?
O make me thine forever;
And should I fainting be,
Lord, let me never, never
Outlive my love to thee.

# At the Cross Her Vigil Keeping

Latin (13th cent.)  8.8.7 D
Trans. *The Hymnal 1982*  *Stabat Mater dolorosa*

At the cross her vigil keeping,
Stood the mournful mother weeping,
Where he hung, the dying Lord:
There she waited in her anguish,
Seeing Christ in torment languish,
In her heart the piercing sword.

With what pain and desolation,
With what grief and resignation,
Mary watched her dying Son.
Deep the woe of her affliction,
When she saw the crucifixion
Of the sole-begotten One.

Him she saw for our salvation
Mocked with cruel acclamation,
Scourged, and crowned with thorns entwined;
Saw him then from judgment taken,
And in death by all forsaken,
Till his spirit he resigned.

Who, on Christ's dear mother gazing,
Pierced by anguish so amazing,
Born of woman, would not weep?
Who, on Christ's dear mother thinking,
Such a cup of sorrow drinking,
Would not share her sorrows deep?

Jesus, may her deep devotion
Stir in me the same emotion,
Fount of love, Redeemer kind;
That my heart fresh ardor gaining,
And a purer love attaining,
May with thee acceptance find.

# When I Survey the Wondrous Cross

Isaac Watts (1707)         LM
                  Galatians 6:14

When I survey the wondrous cross
On which the Prince of glory died,
My richest gain I count but loss,
And pour contempt on all my pride.

Forbid it, Lord, that I should boast,
Save in the death of Christ my God;
All the vain things that charm me most,
I sacrifice them to his blood.

See, from his head, his hands, his feet,
Sorrow and love flow mingled down;
Did e'er such love and sorrow meet,
Or thorns compose so rich a crown?

Were the whole realm of nature mine,
That were a present far too small;
Love so amazing, so divine,
Demands my soul, my life, my all.

## Sing, My Tongue, the Glorious Battle

Venantius Honorius Fortunatus (6th cent.)        8.7.8.7.8.7
Vers. composite        *Pange lingua*

Sing, my tongue, the glorious battle;
Of the mighty conflict sing;
Tell the triumph of the victim,
To his cross thy tribute bring.
Jesus Christ, the world's Redeemer
From that cross now reigns as King.

Thirty years among us dwelling,
His appointed time fulfilled,
Born for this, he meets his passion,
This the Savior freely willed:
On the cross the Lamb is lifted,
Where his precious blood is spilled.

He endures the nails, the spitting,
Vinegar, and spear, and reed;
From that holy body broken
Blood and water forth proceed:
Earth, and stars, and sky, and ocean,
By that flood from stain are freed.

Faithful cross! above all other,
One and only noble tree!
None in foliage, none in blossom,
None in fruit thy peer may be:
Sweetest wood and sweetest iron!
Sweetest weight is hung on thee.

Bend thy boughs, O tree of glory!
Thy relaxing sinews bend;
For awhile the ancient rigor
That thy birth bestowed, suspend;
And the King of heavenly beauty
Gently on thine arms extend.

Praise and honor to the Father,
Praise and honor to the Son,
Praise and honor to the Spirit,
Ever Three and ever One:
One in might and One in glory
While eternal ages run.

## Christ Jesus Lay in Death's Strong Bands

Martin Luther (1524)                       8.7.8.7.7.8.7.4
Trans. Richard Massie (1854)

Christ Jesus lay in death's strong bands,
For our offenses given;
But now at God's right hand he stands
And brings us life from heaven.
Therefore let us joyful be,
And sing to God right thankfully
Loud songs of alleluia!
Alleluia!

It was a strange and dreadful strife
When life and death contended.
The victory remained with life;
The reign of death was ended.
Holy Scripture plainly says
His death has swallowed up our death;
Its sting is lost forever.
Alleluia!

Here the true paschal Lamb we see,
Whom God so freely gave us.
He died on the accursed tree—
So strong his love—to save us.
See, his blood now marks our door;
Faith points to it, death passes o'er,
And Satan cannot harm us.
Alleluia!

So let us keep the festival
To which the Lord invites us.
Christ is himself the joy of all,
The sun that warms and lights us.
Now his grace to us imparts
Eternal sunshine to our hearts;
The night of sin is ended.
Alleluia!

Then let us feast this holy day
On Christ, the bread of heaven.
The word of grace has purged away
The old and evil leaven.
Christ alone our souls will feed;
He is our meat and drink indeed;
Faith lives upon no other!
Alleluia!

## Awake, My Heart, with Gladness

Paul Gerhardt (1648)                                                    7.6.7.6.6.6.6.6
Trans. John Kelly (1867)
  and others

Awake, my heart, with gladness,
See what today is done;
Now, after gloom and sadness,
Comes forth the glorious sun.
My Savior there was laid
Where our bed must be made
When to the realms of light
Our spirit wings its flight.

The foe in triumph shouted
When Christ lay in the tomb;
But, lo, he now is routed,
His boast is turned to gloom,
For Christ again is free;
In glorious victory
He who is strong to save
Has triumphed o'er the grave.

This is a sight that gladdens—
What peace it does impart!
Now nothing ever saddens
The joy within my heart.
No gloom shall ever shake,
No foe shall ever take,
The hope which God's own Son
In love for me has won.

Now hell, its prince, the devil,
Of all their power are shorn;
Now I am safe from evil,
And sin I laugh to scorn.
Grim death with all its might
Cannot my soul affright;
It is a powerless form,
Howe'er it rave and storm.


# Christ the Lord Is Risen Today!

Charles Wesley (1739)                                    7.7.7.7 Alleluias

"Christ the Lord is risen today!" Alleluia!
All creation, join to say; Alleluia!
Raise your joys and triumphs high; Alleluia!
Sing, O heavens, and earth reply, Alleluia!

Love's redeeming work is done, Alleluia!
Fought the fight, the battle won; Alleluia!
Death in vain forbids him rise; Alleluia!
Christ has opened paradise. Alleluia!

Lives again our glorious King; Alleluia!
Where, O death, is now your sting? Alleluia!
Jesus died, our souls to save; Alleluia!
Where your victory, O grave? Alleluia!

Hail, the Lord of earth and heaven! Alleluia!
Praise to you by both be given; Alleluia!
Every knee to you shall bow, Alleluia!
Risen Christ, triumphant now. Alleluia!

# That Easter Day with Joy Was Bright

Latin (5th cent.)                                                                8.8.8.8.4
Trans. John Mason Neale (1851)
  and others

That Easter day with joy was bright;
The sun shone out with fairer light,
When, to their longing eyes restored,
The apostles saw their risen Lord!
Alleluia!

O Jesus, King of gentleness,
With constant love our hearts possess;
To you our lips will ever raise
The tribute of our grateful praise.
Alleluia!

O Christ, you are the Lord of all
In this our Easter festival,
For you will be our strength and shield
From every weapon death can wield.
Alleluia!

All praise, O risen Lord, we give
To you, once dead, but now alive!
To God the Father equal praise,
And God the Holy Ghost, we raise!
Alleluia!

# Sing, Choirs of New Jerusalem

Fulbert of Chartres (early 11th cent.)                        CM
Trans. Robert Campbell (1850)

Sing, choirs of new Jerusalem,
Your sweetest notes employ,
The paschal victory to hymn
In songs of holy joy!

For Judah's Lion burst his chains
And crushed the serpent's head,
Christ cries aloud through death's domains
To wake the imprisoned dead.

Triumphant in his glory now,
To him all power is given,
To him in one communion bow
All saints in earth and heaven.

All glory to the Father be,
All glory to the Son,
All glory to the Spirit be
While endless ages run.

# At the Lamb's High Feast We Sing

Latin (1631)                                                              7.7.7.7.4
Trans. Robert Campbell (1849)

At the Lamb's high feast we sing
Praise to our victorious King,
Who has washed us in the tide
Flowing from his piercèd side.
Alleluia!

Praise we him, whose love divine
Gives his sacred blood for wine,
Gives his body for the feast—
Christ the victim, Christ the priest.
Alleluia!

Where the paschal blood is poured
Death's dread angel sheathes the sword;
Israel's hosts triumphant go
Through the wave that drowns the foe.
Alleluia!

Praise we Christ, whose blood was shed,
Paschal victim, paschal bread;
With sincerity and love
Eat we manna from above.
Alleluia!

Mighty Victim from the sky,
Hell's fierce powers beneath you lie;
You have conquered in the fight,
You have brought us life and light.
Alleluia!

Now no more can death appall,
Now no more the grave enthrall;
You have opened paradise,
And your saints in you shall rise.
Alleluia!

Easter triumph, Easter joy!
This alone can sin destroy;
From sin's power, Lord, set us free,
Newborn souls in you to be.
Alleluia!

Father, who the crown shall give,
Savior, by whose death we live,
Spirit, guide through all our days:
Three in One, your name we praise.
Alleluia!

# On the Day of Resurrection

Michael Peterson (1984)

8.7.8.7
Luke 24:13–35

On the day of resurrection
To Emmaus we return;
While confused, amazed, and frightened,
Jesus comes to us, unknown.

Then this stranger asks a question,
"What is this which troubles you?"
Meets us in our pain and suffering;
Jesus walks with us, unknown.

In our trouble, words come from him;
Burning fire within our hearts
Tells to us the scripture's meaning.
Jesus speaks to us, unknown.

Then we near our destination.
Then we ask the stranger in,
And he yields unto our urging;
Jesus stays with us, unknown.

Day of sorrow is forgotten
When the guest becomes the host.
Taking bread and blessing, breaking,
Jesus is himself made known.

Opened eyes, renewed convictions,
Journey back to scenes of pain;
Telling all that Christ is risen.
Jesus is through us made known.

# Come, Ye Faithful, Raise the Strain

John of Damascus (8th cent.)                                        7.6.7.6 D
Trans. John Mason Neale (1859)

Come, ye faithful, raise the strain
Of triumphant gladness;
God hath brought his Israel
Into joy from sadness;
Loosed from Pharaoh's bitter yoke
Jacob's sons and daughters;
Led them with unmoistened foot
Through the Red Sea waters.

'Tis the spring of souls today;
Christ hath burst his prison,
And from three days sleep in death
As a sun hath risen;
All the winter of our sins,
Long and dark, is flying
From his light, to whom we give
Laud and praise undying.

Now the queen of seasons, bright
With the day of splendor,
With the royal feast of feasts,
Comes its joy to render;
Comes to glad Jerusalem,
Who with true affection
Welcomes in unwearied strains
Jesus' resurrection.

Neither might the gates of death,
Nor the tomb's dark portal,
Nor the watchers, nor the seal
Hold thee as a mortal:
But today amidst thine own
Thou didst stand, bestowing
That thy peace which evermore
Passeth human knowing.

## The Strife Is O'er

Latin (c. 1695)                                           8.8.8 Alleluias
Trans. Francis Pott (1861)

The strife is o'er, the battle done,
The victory of life is won;
The song of triumph has begun.
Alleluia!

The powers of death have done their worst,
But Christ their legions hath dispersed:
Let shouts of holy joy outburst.
Alleluia!

The three sad days are quickly sped,
Christ rises glorious from the dead:
All glory to our risen Head!
Alleluia!

Lord, by your wounds on Calvary
From death's dread sting your servants free,
That we may live eternally.
Alleluia!

# Christ Is Alive! Let Christians Sing

Brian Wren (1968)                                                              LM

Christ is alive! Let Christians sing.
The cross stands empty to the sky.
Let streets and homes with praises ring.
Love, drowned in death, shall never die.

Christ is alive! No longer bound
To distant years in Palestine,
But saving, healing, here and now,
And touching every place and time.

Not throned afar, remotely high,
Untouched, unmoved by human pains,
But daily, in the midst of life,
Our Savior in the Godhead reigns.

In every insult, rift, and war,
Where color, scorn, or wealth divide,
Christ suffers still, yet loves the more,
And lives, where even hope has died.

Christ is alive, and comes to bring
Good news to this and every age,
Till earth and sky and ocean ring
With joy, with justice, love, and praise.

# Hail Thee, Festival Day!

Venantius Honorius Fortunatus (6th cent.)    *Salve festa dies*
Trans. composite

*Easter*
  Hail thee, festival day!
  Blest day to be hallowed forever;
  Day when our Lord was raised,
  Breaking the kingdom of death.

All the fair beauty of earth,
From the death of the winter arising!
Every good gift of the year
Now with its Master returns:

Rise from the grave now, O Lord,
The author of life and creation.
Treading the pathway of death,
New life you give to us all:

*Ascension*
  Hail thee, festival day!
  Blest day to be hallowed forever;
  Day when our risen Lord
  Rose in the heavens to reign.

He who was nailed to the cross
Is ruler and Lord of all people.
All things created on earth
Sing to the glory of God:

(*continued*)

Daily the loveliness grows,
Adorned with the glory of blossom;
Heaven her gates unbars,
Flinging her increase of light:

*Pentecost*
   Hail thee, festival day!
   Blest day to be hallowed forever;
   Day when the Holy Ghost
   Shone in the world with his grace.

Bright and in likeness of fire,
On those who await his appearing,
He whom the Lord had foretold
Suddenly, swiftly descends:

Daily the loveliness grows,
Adorned with the glory of blossom;
Heaven her gates unbars,
Flinging her increase of light:

God the Almighty, the Lord,
The ruler of earth and the heavens
Guard us from harm without;
Cleanse us from evil within:

Jesus, the health of the world,
Enlighten our minds, great Redeemer,
Son of the Father supreme,
Only begotten of God:

Spirit of life and of power,
Now flow in us, fount of our being,
Light that enlightens us all,
Life that in all may abide:

Praise to the giver of good!
O Lover and Author of concord,
Pour out your balm on our days;
Order our ways in your peace:

## Now the Green Blade Rises

John M. C. Crum (1928)                                11.10.10.11
                                        1 Corinthians 15:35–57

Now the green blade rises from the buried grain,
Wheat that in dark earth many days has lain;
Love lives again, that with the dead has been;
Love is come again like wheat arising green.

In the grave they laid him, Love by hatred slain,
Thinking that he would never wake again,
Laid in the earth like grain that sleeps unseen;
Love is come again like wheat arising green.

Forth he came at Easter, like the risen grain,
He that for three days in the grave had lain;
Raised from the dead, my living Lord is seen;
Love is come again like wheat arising green.

When our hearts are wintry, grieving, or in pain,
Your touch can call us back to life again,
Fields of our hearts that dead and bare have been;
Love is come again like wheat arising green.

# O Sons and Daughters, Let Us Sing!

Attr. Jean Tisserand (15th cent.)                                    8.8.8 Alleluias
Trans. John Mason Neale (1852)                                      John 20:11–29

O sons and daughters, let us sing!
The King of heaven, the glorious King,
O'er death today rose triumphing.
Alleluia!

That Easter morn, at break of day,
The faithful women went their way
To seek the tomb where Jesus lay.
Alleluia!

An angel clad in white they see,
Who sat, and spake unto the three,
"Your Lord doth go to Galilee."
Alleluia!

That night the apostles met in fear;
Amidst them came their Lord most dear,
And said, "My peace be on all here."
Alleluia!

When Thomas first the tidings heard,
How they had seen the risen Lord,
He doubted the disciples' word.
Alleluia!

"My piercèd side, O Thomas, see;
My hands, my feet, I show to thee;
Not faithless, but believing be."
Alleluia!

No longer Thomas then denied,
He saw the feet, the hands, the side;
"Thou art my Lord and God," he cried.
Alleluia!

How blest are they who have not seen,
And yet whose faith has constant been,
For they eternal life shall win.
Alleluia!

On this most holy day of days,
To God your hearts and voices raise,
In laud, and jubilee, and praise.
Alleluia!

## Alleluia! Sing to Jesus!

William Chatterton Dix (1866)                                    8.7.8.7 D

Alleluia! Sing to Jesus!
His the scepter, his the throne!
Alleluia! his the triumph,
His the victory alone!
Hark! the songs of peaceful Zion
Thunder like a mighty flood;
Jesus out of every nation
Hath redeemed us by his blood.

Alleluia! Not as orphans
Are we left in sorrow now.
Alleluia! he is near us;
Faith believes nor questions how.
Though the cloud from sight received him,
When the forty days were o'er,
Shall our hearts forget his promise,
''I am with you evermore''?

Alleluia! Bread of angels,
Thou on earth our food, our stay.
Alleluia! Here the sinful
Flee to thee from day to day.
Intercessor, friend of sinners,
Earth's Redeemer, plead for me,
Where the songs of all the sinless
Sweep across the crystal sea.

Alleluia! King eternal,
Thee the Lord of lords we own;
Alleluia! Born of Mary,
Earth thy footstool, heaven thy throne.
Thou within the veil hast entered,
Robed in flesh, our great High Priest;
Thou on earth both Priest and Victim
In the eucharistic feast.

# The Head That Once Was Crowned

Thomas Kelly (1820)                                        CM
                                                   Hebrews 2:9

The head that once was crowned with thorns
Is crowned with glory now;
A royal diadem adorns
The mighty victor's brow.

The highest place that heaven affords
Is his, is his by right,
The King of kings, and Lord of lords,
And heaven's eternal Light:

The joy of all who dwell above,
The joy of all below
To whom he manifests his love,
And grants his name to know.

To them the cross, with all its shame,
With all its grace, is given;
Their name an everlasting name,
Their joy the joy of heaven.

They suffer with their Lord below,
They reign with him above;
Their profit and their joy to know
The wonder of his love.

# A Hymn of Glory Let Us Sing

The Venerable Bede (early 8th cent.)                    LM
Sts. 1–2 trans. Elizabeth Rundle Charles (1858)
St. 3 trans. Benjamin Webb (1854)

A hymn of glory let us sing,
New hymns throughout the world shall ring;
By a new way none ever trod
Christ takes his place, the throne of God!

You are a present joy, O Lord,
You will be ever our reward,
And great the light in you we see
To guide us to eternity.

O risen Christ, ascended Lord,
All praise to you let earth accord.
You are, while endless ages run,
With Father and with Spirit one.

# At the Name of Jesus

Caroline Maria Noel (1870)

6.5.6.5 D
Philippians 2:5–11

At the name of Jesus
Every knee shall bow,
Every tongue confess him
King of glory now:
'Tis the Father's pleasure
We should call him Lord,
Who from the beginning
Was the mighty Word.

Humbled for a season,
To receive a name
From the lips of sinners,
Unto whom he came,
Faithfully he bore it
Spotless to the last,
Brought it back victorious,
When from death he passed;

Bore it up triumphant,
With its human light,
Through all ranks of creatures,
To the central height,
To the throne of Godhead,
To the Father's breast;
Filled it with the glory
Of that perfect rest.

Name him, Christians, name him,
With love strong as death,
Name with awe and wonder
And with bated breath;
He is God the Savior,
He is Christ the Lord,
Ever to be worshiped,
Trusted, and adored.

In your hearts enthrone him;
There let him subdue
All that is not holy,
All that is not true;
Crown him as your Captain
In temptation's hour;
Let his will enfold you
In its light and power.

Christians, this Lord Jesus
Shall return again,
With his Father's glory
O'er the earth to reign;
For all wreaths of empire
Meet upon his brow,
And our hearts confess him
King of glory now.

## Crown Him with Many Crowns

Matthew Bridges (1851)                                                    SMD

Crown him with many crowns,
The Lamb upon his throne;
Hark, how the heavenly anthem drowns
All music but its own!
Awake, my soul, and sing
Of him who died for thee,
And hail him as thy matchless King
Through all eternity.

Crown him the Lord of love;
Behold his hands and side,
Rich wounds, yet visible above,
In beauty glorified:
No angel in the sky
Can fully bear that sight,
But downward bends his burning eye
At mysteries so bright.

Crown him the Lord of peace;
Whose power a scepter sways
From pole to pole, that wars may cease,
Absorbed in prayer and praise:
His reign shall know no end;
And round his piercèd feet
Fair flowers of paradise extend
Their fragrance ever sweet.

Crown him the Lord of years,
The Potentate of time;
Creator of the rolling spheres,
Ineffably sublime.
All hail, Redeemer, hail!
For thou hast died for me;
Thy praise shall never, never fail
Throughout eternity.

## Rejoice, the Lord Is King!

Charles Wesley (1746)                          6.6.6.6.8.8

Rejoice, the Lord is King!
Your Lord and King adore!
Rejoice, give thinks, and sing,
And triumph evermore:
Lift up your heart, lift up your voice!
Rejoice, again I say, rejoice!

God's kingdom cannot fail,
Christ rules o'er earth and heaven;
The keys of death and hell
Are to our Jesus given:
Lift up your heart, lift up your voice!
Rejoice, again I say, rejoice!

Rejoice in glorious hope!
For Christ, the Judge, shall come
To glorify the saints
For their eternal home:
Lift up your heart, lift up your voice!
Rejoice, again I say, rejoice!

# Earth's Scattered Isles and Contoured Hills

Jeffery Rowthorn (1974)                              8.8.8.8.8.8
                                                      Psalm 97

Earth's scattered isles and contoured hills
Which part the seas and mold the land,
And vistas newly seen from space
That show a world awesome and grand,
All wondrously unite to sing:
Take heart, take hope, the Lord is King!

God's judgment passed on social ills
That thwart awhile divine intent,
The flagging dreams of weary folk
Whose brave new world lies torn and rent,
In painful form their message bring:
Take heart, take hope, the Lord is King!

The constant care which Israel knew
Alike in faith and faithlessness,
The subtle providence which guides
A pilgrim church through change and stress,
Inspire us gratefully to sing:
Take heart, take hope, the Lord is King!

The light which shines through noble acts,
The quest for truth dispelling lies,
The grace of Christ renewed in us
So love lives on and discord dies,
All blend their song, good news to bring:
Take heart, take hope, the Lord is king!

# All Praise to Thee, for Thou, O King Divine

F. Bland Tucker (1938)                                    10.10.10 Alleluias
                                                          Philippians 2:5–11

All praise to thee, for thou, O King divine,
Didst yield the glory that of right was thine,
That in our darkened hearts thy grace might shine:
Alleluia!

Thou cam'st to us in lowliness of thought;
By thee the outcast and the poor were sought,
And by thy death was God's salvation wrought:
Alleluia!

Let this mind be in us which was in thee,
Who wast a servant, that we might be free,
Humbling thyself to death on Calvary:
Alleluia!

Wherefore, by God's eternal purpose, thou
Art high exalted o'er all creatures now,
And given the name to which all knees shall bow:
Alleluia!

Let every tongue confess with one accord
In heaven and earth that Jesus Christ is Lord;
And God the Father be by all adored:
Alleluia!

# Jesus Shall Reign Where'er the Sun

Isaac Watts (1719)
LM
Psalm 72

Jesus shall reign where'er the sun
Does its successive journeys run,
His kingdom stretch from shore to shore,
Till moons shall wax and wane no more.

To him shall endless prayer be made,
And praises throng to crown his head;
His name, like sweet perfume, shall rise
With every morning sacrifice.

People and realms of every tongue
Dwell on his love with sweetest song,
And infant voices shall proclaim
Their early blessings on his name.

Blessings abound where'er he reigns;
The prisoners leap to lose their chains,
The weary find eternal rest,
And all who suffer want are blest.

Let every creature rise and bring
Honors peculiar to our King;
Angels descend with songs again,
And earth repeat the loud Amen!

# As the Bridegroom to His Chosen

Attr. John Tauler (14th cent.)                                    8.7.8.7.6
Trans. Emma Frances Bevan (c. 1858)

As the bridegroom to his chosen,
As the king unto his realm,
As the keep unto the castle,
As the pilot to the helm,
So, Lord, art thou to me.

As the fountain in the garden,
As the candle in the dark,
As the treasure in the coffer,
As the manna in the ark,
So, Lord, art thou to me.

As the music at the banquet,
As the stamp unto the seal,
As the medicine to the fainting,
As the winecup at the meal,
So, Lord, are thou to me.

As the ruby in the setting,
As the honey in the comb,
As the light within the lantern,
As the father in the home,
So, Lord, art thou to me.

As the sunshine in the heavens
As the image in the glass,
As the fruit unto the fig tree,
As the dew upon the grass,
So, Lord, art thou to me.

# Beautiful Savior

*Münster Gesangbuch* (1677)                                    5.5.7.5.5.8
Trans. Joseph Augustus Seiss (1873)

Beautiful Savior,
King of creation,
Son of God and Son of Man!
Truly I'd love thee,
Truly I'd serve thee,
Light of my soul, my joy, my crown.

Fair are the meadows,
Fair are the woodlands,
Robed in flowers of blooming spring;
Jesus is fairer,
Jesus is purer;
He makes our sorrowing spirit sing.

Fair is the sunshine,
Fair is the moonlight,
Bright the sparkling stars on high;
Jesus shines brighter,
Jesus shines purer
Than all the angels in the sky.

Beautiful Savior,
Lord of the nations,
Son of God and Son of Man!
Glory and honor,
Praise, adoration
Now and forevermore be thine!

## Christ, You Are the Fullness

Vers. Bert Polman (1986)                    Colossians 1:15–18; 3:1–4, 15–17

Christ, you are the fullness of God, firstborn of
    everything.
For by you all things were made; you hold them up.
You are head of the church, which is your body.
Firstborn from the dead, you in all things are supreme!

Since we have been raised with you, Lord, help keep our
    hearts and minds
Pure and set on things that build your rule o'er all the
    earth.
All our life is now hidden with you in God.
When you come again, we will share your glory.

Help us live in peace as true members of your body.
Let your word dwell richly in us as we teach and sing.
Thanks and praise be to God through you, Lord Jesus.
In whate'er we do let your name receive the praise!

# I Greet Thee, Who My Sure Redeemer Art

French Psalter, Strassburg (1545)                                    10.10.10.10
Trans. Elizabeth L. Smith (1868)

I greet thee, who my sure Redeemer art,
My only trust and Savior of my heart,
Who pain didst undergo for my poor sake;
I pray thee from our hearts all cares to take.

Thou art the King of mercy and of grace,
Reigning omnipotent in every place:
So come, O King, and our whole being sway;
Shine on us with the light of thy pure day.

Thou art the life, by which alone we live,
And all our substance and our strength receive;
Sustain us by thy faith and by thy power,
And give us strength in every trying hour.

Thou hast the true and perfect gentleness,
No harshness hast thou and no bitterness:
O grant to us the grace we find in thee,
That we may dwell in perfect unity.

Our hope is in no other save in thee;
Our faith is built upon thy promise free;
Lord, give us peace, and make us calm and sure,
That in thy strength we evermore endure.

# We Sing the Praise of Him Who Died

Thomas Kelly (1815)                                    LM

We sing the praise of him who died,
Of him who died upon the cross.
The sinner's hope let all deride;
For this we count the world but loss.

Inscribed upon the cross we see
In shining letters, "God is love."
He bears our sins upon the tree;
He brings us mercy from above.

The cross! It takes our guilt away;
It holds the fainting spirit up;
It cheers with hope the gloomy day
And sweetens every bitter cup.

It makes the coward spirit brave
And nerves the feeble arm for fight;
It takes the terror from the grave
And gilds the bed of death with light;

The balm of life, the cure of woe,
The measure and the pledge of love,
The sinner's refuge here below,
The angels' theme in heaven above.

# O for a Thousand Tongues to Sing

Charles Wesley (1739)          CM

O for a thousand tongues to sing
My great Redeemer's praise,
The glories of my God and King,
The triumphs of his grace!

My gracious Master and my God,
Assist me to proclaim,
To spread through all the earth abroad
The honors of thy name.

Jesus! the name that charms our fears,
That bids our sorrows cease;
'Tis music in the sinner's ears,
'Tis life, and health, and peace.

He breaks the power of canceled sin,
He sets the prisoner free;
His blood can make the foulest clean;
His blood availed for me.

He speaks, and listening to his voice,
New life the dead receive;
The mournful, broken hearts rejoice,
The humble poor believe.

Hear him, ye deaf; his praise, ye dumb,
Your loosened tongues employ;
Ye blind, behold your Savior come,
And leap, ye lame, for joy.

In Christ, your head, you then shall know,
Shall feel your sins forgiven;
Anticipate your heaven below,
And own that love is heaven.

## Blessed Jesus, at Your Word

Tobias Clausnitzer (1663)                          7.8.7.8.8.8
Trans. Catherine Winkworth (1858)

Blessed Jesus, at your word
We are gathered all to hear you;
Let our hearts and souls be stirred
Now to seek and love and fear you;
By your teachings true and holy,
Drawn from earth to love you solely.

All our knowledge, sense, and sight
Lie in deepest darkness shrouded,
Till your Spirit breaks our night
With the beams of truth unclouded;
You alone to God can win us,
You must work all good within us.

Glorious Lord, yourself impart!
Light of light, from God proceeding,
Open now our ears and heart,
Help us by your Spirit's pleading;
Hear the cry that we are raising;
Hear, and bless our prayers and praising.

# Christ Is the World's Light

Fred Pratt Green (1968)                                    10.11.11.6

Christ is the world's light, Christ and none other;
Born in our darkness, he became our brother.
If we have seen him, we have seen the Father:
Glory to God on high!

Christ is the world's peace, Christ and none other;
No one can serve him and despise another.
Who else unites us, one in God the Father?
Glory to God on high!

Christ is the world's life, Christ and none other;
Sold once for silver, murdered here, our brother;
He, who redeems us, reigns with God the Father:
Glory to God on high!

Give God the glory, God and none other;
Give God the glory, Spirit, Son, and Father;
Give God the glory, God with us, my brother:
Glory to God on high!

# We Come, O Christ, to You

Margaret Clarkson (1946, 1984) 6.6.6.6.8.8

We come, O Christ, to you,
True Son of God and man;
By whom all things consist,
In whom all life began:
In you alone we live and move.
And have our being in your love.

You are the Way to God,
Your blood our ransom paid;
In you we face our Judge
And Maker unafraid;
Before the throne absolved we stand:
Your love has met your law's demand.

You are the living Truth,
All wisdom dwells in you,
The source of every skill,
The One eternal TRUE!
O great I AM! in you we rest,
Sure answer to our every quest.

You only are true Life,
To know you is to live
The more abundant life
That earth can never give.
O risen Lord! we live in you:
In us each day your life renew!

(*continued*)

We worship you, Lord Christ,
Our Savior and our King;
To you our youth and strength
Adoringly we bring:
So fill our hearts that all may view
Your life in us, and turn to you!

## Like the Murmur of the Dove's Song

Carl P. Daw, Jr. (1982)                                    8.7.8.7.6

Like the murmur of the dove's song,
Like the challenge of her flight,
Like the vigor of the wind's rush,
Like the new flame's eager might:
Come, Holy Spirit, come.

To the members of Christ's body,
To the branches of the Vine,
To the church in faith assembled,
To her midst as gift and sign:
Come, Holy Spirit, come.

With the healing of division,
With the ceaseless voice of prayer,
With the power to love and witness,
With the peace beyond compare:
Come, Holy Spirit, come.

# Come Down, O Love Divine

Bianco da Siena (early 15th cent.)                                    6.6.11 D
Trans. Richard Frederick Littledale (1867)

Come down, O Love divine,
Seek out this soul of mine
And visit it with your own ardor glowing;
O Comforter, draw near,
Within my heart appear,
And kindle it, your holy flame bestowing.

O let it freely burn,
Till earthly passions turn
To dust and ashes in its heat consuming;
And let your glorious light
Shine ever on my sight,
And clothe me round, the while my path illuming.

And so the yearning strong
With which the soul will long
Shall far outpass the power of human telling;
For none can guess God's grace,
Till Love creates a place
Wherein the Holy Spirit makes a dwelling.

# Come, Holy Ghost, God and Lord

Latin (12th cent.)                                    7.8.8.8.8.8.8.8.10.8
St. 1, German (15th cent.)                        *Veni Sancte Spiritus*
Sts. 2–3, Martin Luther (1524)
Trans. *The Lutheran Hymnal* (1941)


Come, Holy Ghost, God and Lord,
With all your graces now outpoured
On each believer's mind and heart;
Your fervent love to them impart.
Lord, by the brightness of your light
In holy faith your church unite;
From every land and every tongue,
This to your praise, O Lord, our God, be sung:
Alleluia! Alleluia!


Come, holy Light, Guide divine,
Now cause the Word of life to shine.
Teach us to know our God aright
And call him Father with delight.
From every error keep us free;
Let none but Christ our Master be,
That we in living faith abide,
In him, our Lord, with all our might confide.
Alleluia! Alleluia!


Come, holy Fire, comfort true,
Grant us the will your work to do
And in your service to abide;
Let trials turn us not aside.

Lord, by your power prepare each heart
And to our weakness strength impart,
That bravely here we may contend,
Through life and death to you, our Lord, ascend.
Alleluia! Alleluia!

## Holy Ghost, Dispel Our Sadness

Paul Gerhardt (1648)                                              8.7.8.7 D
Trans. John Christian Jacobi (c. 1725)

Holy Ghost, dispel our sadness;
Pierce the clouds of nature's night;
Come, O source of joy and gladness,
Breathe your life, and spread your light.
From the height which knows no measure,
As a gracious shower descend,
Bringing down the richest treasure
We can wish, or God can send.

Author of the new creation,
Come, anoint us with your power.
Make our hearts your habitation;
With your grace our spirits shower.
Hear, O hear our supplication,
Blessed Spirit, God of peace!
Rest upon this congregation
With the fullness of your grace.

# Come, Holy Spirit, Our Souls Inspire

Attr. Rabanus Maurus (9th cent.)                                    LM
Trans. John Cosin (1627)                              *Veni Creator Spiritus*

Come, Holy Spirit, our souls inspire,
And lighten with celestial fire.

Thou the anointing Spirit art,
Who dost thy sevenfold gifts impart.

Thy blessèd unction from above
Is comfort, life, and fire of love.

Enable with perpetual light
The dullness of our blinded sight.

Anoint and cheer our soiled face
With the abundance of thy grace.

Keep far our foes, give peace at home:
Where thou art guide, no ill can come.

Teach us to know the Father, Son,
And thee, of both, to be but One,

That through the ages all along,
This may be our endless song:

Praise to thy eternal merit,
Father, Son, and Holy Spirit.

# Come, Holy Spirit, Heavenly Dove

Isaac Watts (1707)                                        CM

Come, Holy Spirit, heavenly Dove,
With all thy quickening powers;
Kindle a flame of sacred love
In these cold hearts of ours.

In vain we tune our formal songs,
In vain we strive to rise;
Hosannas languish on our tongues,
And our devotion dies.

Dear Lord, and shall we ever live
At this poor dying rate?
Our love so faint, so cold to thee,
And thine to us so great!

Come, Holy Spirit, heavenly Dove,
With all thy quickening powers;
Come, shed abroad a Savior's love,
And that shall kindle ours.

# For Your Gift of God the Spirit

Margaret Clarkson (1959, 1984)        8.7.8.7 D

For your gift of God the Spirit,
Power to make our lives anew,
Pledge of life and hope of glory,
Savior, we would worship you.
Crowning gift of resurrection
Sent from your ascended throne,
Fullness of the very Godhead,
Come to make your life our own.

He who in creation's dawning
Brooded on the lifeless deep,
Still across our nature's darkness
Moves to wake our souls from sleep.
Moves to stir, to draw, to quicken,
Thrusts us through with sense of sin;
Brings to birth and seals and fills us—
Saving Advocate within.

He, himself the living Author,
Wakes to life the sacred Word,
Reads with us its holy pages
And reveals our risen Lord.
He it is who works within us,
Teaching rebel hearts to pray,
He whose holy intercessions
Rise for us both night and day.

He, the mighty God, indwells us;
His to strengthen, help, empower;
His to overcome the tempter—
Ours to call in danger's hour.
In his strength we dare to battle
All the raging hosts of sin,
And by him alone we conquer
Foes without and foes within.

Father, grant your Holy Spirit
In our hearts may rule today,
Grieved not, quenched not, but unhindered,
Work in us his sovereign way.
Fill us with your holy fullness,
God the Father, Spirit, Son:
In us, through us, then, forever,
Shall your perfect will be done.

# O Spirit of the Living God

James Montgomery (1823)                        LM

O Spirit of the living God,
In all the fullness of your grace,
Wherever human feet have trod,
Descend on our apostate race.

Give tongues of fire and hearts of love
To preach the reconciling Word;
Give power and unction from above,
Where'er this blessed sound is heard.

Be darkness, at your coming, light;
Confusion, order in your path;
Souls without strength inspire with might;
Let mercy triumph over wrath.

O Spirit of the Lord, prepare
A sinful world its God to meet;
And breathe abroad like morning air,
Till hearts of stone begin to beat.

Proclaim the gospel far and wide;
The triumphs of the cross record;
The name of Christ be glorified;
Let every people call him Lord!

# Of All the Spirit's Gifts to Me

Fred Pratt Green (1979)                                    8.8.8.4

Of all the Spirit's gifts to me,
I pray that I may never cease
To take and treasure most these three:
Love, joy, and peace.

The Spirit shows me love's the root
Of every gift sent from above,
Of every flower, of every fruit,
That God is love.

The Spirit shows if I possess
A love no evil can destroy;
However great is my distress,
Then this is joy.

Though what's ahead is mystery,
And life itself is ours on lease,
Each day the Spirit says to me,
"Go forth in peace!"

We go in peace, but made aware
That, in a needy world like this,
Our clearest purpose is to share
Love, joy, and peace.

# Spirit of God, Descend upon My Heart

George Croly (1867)　　　　　　　　　　　　　　　10.10.10.10

Spirit of God, descend upon my heart;
Wean it from earth, through all its pulses move;
Stoop to my weakness, mighty as thou art,
And make me love thee as I ought to love.

I ask no dream, no prophet ecstasies,
No sudden rending of the veil of clay,
No angel visitant, no opening skies;
But take the dimness of my soul away.

Hast thou not bid us love thee, God and King;
All, all thine own: soul, heart, and strength, and mind?
I see thy cross, there teach my heart to cling.
O let me seek thee, and O let me find!

Teach me to feel that thou art always nigh;
Teach me the struggles of the soul to bear,
To check the rising doubt, the rebel sigh;
Teach me the patience of unanswered prayer.

Teach me to love thee as thine angels love,
One holy passion filling all my frame;
The baptism of the heaven-descended Dove,
My heart an altar, and thy love the flame.

# Christ Is Made the Sure Foundation

Latin (7th cent.)                                    8.7.8.7.8.7
Trans. John Mason Neale (1851)

Christ is made the sure foundation,
Christ the head and cornerstone;
Chosen of the Lord and precious,
Binding all the church in one;
Holy Zion's help forever,
And her confidence alone.

To this temple, where we call thee,
Come, O Lord of Hosts, today!
With thy faithful lovingkindness
Hear thy people as they pray,
And thy fullest benediction
Shed within its walls alway.

Here vouchsafe to all thy servants
What they ask of thee to gain;
What they gain from thee forever
With the blessed to retain,
And hereafter in thy glory
Evermore with thee to reign.

Laud and honor to the Father,
Laud and honor to the Son,
Laud and honor to the Spirit,
Ever three and ever one;
One in might and one in glory,
While unending ages run.

## Built on a Rock

Nikolai F. S. Grundtvig (1837, 1854)        8.8.8.8.8.8.8
Trans. Carl Doving (1909)

Built on a rock the church doth stand,
Even when steeples are falling;
Crumbled have spires in every land,
Bells still are chiming and calling;
Calling the young and old to rest,
Calling the souls of men distressed,
Longing for life everlasting.

Not in our temples made with hands
God the Almighty, is dwelling;
High in the heavens his temple stands,
All earthly temples excelling;
Yet he who dwells in heaven above
Deigns to abide with us in love,
Making our bodies his temple.

We are God's house of living stones,
Built for his own habitation;
He fills our hearts, his humble thrones,
Granting us life and salvation;
Were two or three to seek his face,
He in their midst would show his grace,
Blessings upon them bestowing.

Yet in this house, an earthly frame,
Jesus the children is blessing;
Hither we come to praise his name,
Faith in our Savior confessing;
Jesus to us his Spirit sent,
Making with us his covenant,
Granting his children the kingdom.

Through all the passing years, O Lord,
Grant that, when church bells are ringing,
Many may come to hear God's Word
Where he this promise is bringing:
"I know mine own, mine own know me,
Ye, not the world, my face shall see;
My peace I leave with you. Amen."

# Christian Hearts, in Love United

Nicolaus L. von Zinzendorf (1723)                          8.7.8.7 D
Trans. composite

Christian hearts, in love united,
Search to know God's holy will,
Let his love, in us ignited,
More and more your spirits fill.
Christ the Head, and we his members—
We reflect the light he is.
Christ the Master, we disciples—
He is ours and we are his.

Grant, Lord, that with your direction,
"Love each other," we comply.
Help us live in true affection,
Your love to exemplify.
Let our mutual love be glowing
Brightly so that all may know
That we, as on one stem growing,
Living branches are in you.

Come, then, living church of Jesus,
Covenant with him anew.
Unto him who conquered for us
Let us pledge our service true.
Let our lives reflect the brightness
Of God's love in Jesus shown.
To the world we then bear witness:
We belong to God alone.

# Glorious Things of Thee Are Spoken

John Newton (1779)                                    8.7.8.7 D
                                                      Psalm 87

Glorious things of thee are spoken,
Zion, city of our God;
God, whose word cannot be broken,
Formed thee for a blest abode.
On the rock of ages founded,
What can shake thy sure repose?
With salvation's wall surrounded,
Thou may'st smile at all thy foes.

See, the streams of living waters,
Springing from eternal love,
Well supply thy sons and daughters
And all fear of want remove.
Who can faint while such a river
Ever flows their thirst to assuage?
Grace, which like the Lord the giver,
Never fails from age to age.

Round each habitation hovering,
See the cloud and fire appear
For a glory and a covering,
Showing that the Lord is near.
Thus deriving from their banner
Light by night and shade by day,
Safe they feed upon the manna
Which God gives them when they pray.

# God Is Here!

Fred Pratt Green (1979, 1988) 8.7.8.7 D

God is here! As we your people
Meet to offer praise and prayer,
May we find in fuller measure
What it is in Christ we share.
Here, as in the world around us,
All our varied skills and arts
Wait the coming of the Spirit
Into open minds and hearts.

Here are symbols to remind us
Of our lifelong need of grace;
Here are table, font, and pulpit;
Here the cross has central place.
Here in honesty of preaching,
Here in silence, as in speech,
Here, in newness and renewal,
God the Spirit comes to each.

Here our children find a welcome
In the Shepherd's flock and fold,
Here, as bread and wine are taken,
Christ sustains us as of old.
Here the servants of the Servant
Seek in worship to explore
What it means in daily living
To believe and to adore.

Lord of all, of church and kingdom,
In an age of change and doubt
Keep us faithful to the gospel,
Help us work your purpose out.
Here, in this day's dedication,
All we have to give, receive:
We, who cannot live without you,
We adore you! We believe!

# In Christ There Is No East or West

John Oxenham (1908)                                            CM

In Christ there is no east or west,
In him no south or north;
But one great fellowship of love
Throughout the whole wide earth.

In Christ shall true hearts everywhere
Their high communion find;
His service is the golden cord
Close-binding humankind.

Join hands, disciples of the faith,
Whate'er your race may be.
All children of the living God
Are surely kin to me.

In Christ now meet both east and west,
In him meet south and north;
All Christly souls are one in him
Throughout the whole wide earth.

# Living Word of God Eternal

Jeffery Rowthorn (1983)

8.7.8.7.8.7
Acts 2:42

Living Word of God eternal,
Laying claim to every age,
Jesus, speak through all our speaking,
Bring to life the Bible's page;
Let your gospel, heard and heeded,
Set our course of pilgrimage.

Loving Savior, whose embraces
Our true selves alone unmask,
In this fellowship's small compass
Train us for our common task:
By our love to grow more like you
And to dare what you will ask.

Living Bread come down from heaven,
Broken, shared, distributed,
Feed us, gathered at this table,
With your grace unlimited,
And as servants then employ us
Till this hungry world is fed.

Loving Spirit, praying in us,
Giving voice to all our sighs,
Show the wideness of your mercy
To deaf ears and blinded eyes;
Free our tongues to come before you
With our neighbors' joys and cries.

May your Word among us spoken,
May the loving which we dare,
May your Bread among us broken,
May the prayers in which we share
Daily make us faithful people,
Living signs, Lord, of your care.

# The Church's One Foundation

Samuel John Stone (1866)                                        7.6.7.6 D

The church's one foundation
Is Jesus Christ her Lord;
She is his new creation
By water and the word;
From heaven he came and sought her
To be his holy bride;
With his own blood he bought her,
And for her life he died.

Elect from every nation,
Yet one o'er all the earth,
Her charter of salvation
One Lord, one faith, one birth;
One holy name she blesses,
Partakes one holy food,
And to one hope she presses,
With every grace endued.

Though with a scornful wonder
This world sees her oppressed,
By schisms rent asunder,
By heresies distressed,
Yet saints their watch are keeping;
Their cry goes up: "How long?"
And soon the night of weeping
Shall be the morn of song.

Mid toil and tribulation,
And tumult of her war,
She waits the consummation
Of peace forevermore;
Till with the vision glorious
Her longing eyes are blest,
And the great church victorious
Shall be the church at rest.

Yet she on earth has union
With God the Three in One,
And mystic sweet communion
With those whose rest is won:
O happy ones and holy!
Lord, give us grace that we,
Like them, the meek and lowly,
May live eternally.

# Thanks to God Whose Word Was Spoken

R. T. Brooks (1954)                                                    8.7.8.7.4.4.7

> Thanks to God whose Word was spoken
> In the deed that made the earth;
> His the voice that called a nation,
> His the fires that tried her worth.
> God has spoken, God has spoken:
> Praise him for his open Word!
>
> Thanks to God whose Word incarnate
> Human flesh has glorified,
> Who by life and death and rising
> Grace abundant has supplied.
> God has spoken, God has spoken:
> Praise him for his open Word!
>
> Thanks to God whose Word was written
> On the Bible's sacred page,
> Record of the revelation
> Showing God to every age.
> God has spoken, God has spoken:
> Praise him for his open Word!
>
> Thanks to God whose Word is published
> In the tongues of every race;
> See its glory undiminished
> By the change of time or place,
> God is speaking, God is speaking:
> Praise him for his open Word!

Thanks to God whose Word is answered
By the Spirit's voice within;
Here we drink of joy unmeasured,
Life redeemed from death and sin.
God is speaking, God is speaking;
Praise him for his open Word!

## Break Thou the Bread of Life

Mary A. Lathbury (1877)                                    6.4.6.4 D

Break thou the bread of life,
Dear Lord, to me,
As thou didst break the loaves
Beside the sea;
Beyond the sacred page
I seek thee, Lord;
My spirit pants for thee,
O living Word!

Bless thou the truth, dear Lord,
Now unto me,
As thou didst bless the bread
By Galilee;
Then shall all bondage cease,
All fetters fall;
And I shall find my peace,
My all in all.

# O Word of God Incarnate

William Walsham How (1867)                                      7.6.7.6 D

O Word of God incarnate,
O Wisdom from on high,
O Truth unchanged, unchanging,
O Light of our dark sky:
We praise you for the radiance
That from the hallowed page,
A lantern to our footsteps,
Shines on from age to age.

The church from you, dear Savior,
Received this gift divine,
And still that light is lifted
On all the earth to shine.
It is the chart and compass
That, all life's voyage through,
Amid the rocks and quicksands,
Still guides, O Christ, to you.

O make your church, dear Savior,
A lamp of purest gold
To bear before the nations
Your true light, as of old;
O teach your wandering pilgrims
By this our path to trace,
Till, clouds and storms thus ended,
We see you face to face.

# All Who Believe and Are Baptized

Thomas H. Kingo (1689)                                    8.7.8.7.8.8.7
Trans. George T. Rygh (1909)

All who believe and are baptized
Shall see the Lord's salvation;
Baptized into the death of Christ,
They are a new creation;
Through Christ's redemption they will stand
Among the glorious heavenly band
Of every tribe and nation.

With one accord, O God, we pray,
Grant us Your Holy Spirit;
Help us in our infirmity
Through Jesus' blood and merit;
Grant us to grow in grace each day
By holy Baptism, that we may
Eternal life inherit.

# Baptized in Water

Michael Saward (1981)　　　　　　　　　　　　　　　5.5.8 D

Baptized in water,
Sealed by the Spirit,
Cleansed by the blood of Christ, our King;
Heirs of salvation,
Trusting his promise,
Faithfully now God's praise we sing.

Baptized in water,
Sealed by the Spirit,
Dead in the tomb with Christ, our King;
One with his rising,
Freed and forgiven,
Thankfully now God's praise we sing.

Baptized in water,
Sealed by the Spirit,
Marked with the sign of Christ, our King;
Born of one Father,
We are his children,
Joyfully now God's praise we sing.

# Dearest Jesus, We Are Here

Benjamin Schmolck (1704)                                    7.8.7.8.8.8
Trans. Catherine Winkworth (1858)

Dearest Jesus, we are here,
Gladly your command obeying.
With this child we now draw near
In response to your own saying
That to you it shall be given
As a child and heir of heaven.

Your command is clear and plain,
And we would obey it duly:
"You must all be born again,
Heart and life renewing truly,
Born of water and the Spirit,
And my kingdom thus inherit."

This is why we come to you,
In our arms this infant bearing;
Lord, to us your glory show;
Let this child, your mercy sharing,
In your arms be shielded ever,
Yours on earth and yours forever.

Gracious Lord, your member own;
Shepherd, take your lamb and feed it;
Prince of Peace, make here your throne;
Way of life, to heaven lead it;
Precious vine, let nothing sever
From your side this branch forever.

# We Know That Christ Is Raised

John Brownlow Geyer (1969)                            10.10.10.4
Romans 6:3–9

We know that Christ is raised and dies no more.
Embraced by death he broke its fearful hold;
And our despair he turned to blazing joy.
Alleluia!

We share by water in his saving death.
Reborn we share with him an Easter life
As living members of a living Christ.
Alleluia!

The Father's splendor clothes the Son with life.
The Spirit's power shakes the church of God.
Baptized we live with God the Three in One.
Alleluia!

A new creation comes to life and grows
As Christ's new body takes on flesh and blood.
The universe, restored and whole, will sing:
Alleluia!

## Deck Yourself, My Soul, with Gladness

Johann Franck (1653)                                    LMD
Trans. Catherine Winkworth (1863)
  and John Casper Mattes (1913)

Deck yourself, my soul, with gladness,
Leave behind all gloom and sadness;
Come into the daylight's splendor,
There with joy your praises render
Unto God, whose grace unbounded
Has this wondrous banquet founded;
Come, for now the Lord most holy
Stoops to you in likeness lowly.

Sun, who all my life does brighten;
Light, who does my soul enlighten;
Joy, your wondrous gift bestowing;
Fount, from which all good is flowing:
At your feet I cry, my Maker,
Let me be a fit partaker
Of this blessed food from heaven,
For our good, your glory given.

Jesus, source of life and pleasure,
Truest friend and dearest treasure,
By your love I am invited,
Be your love with love requited.
From this banquet let me measure,
Lord, how vast and deep its treasure;
Through the gifts that here you give me,
As your guest in heaven receive me.

# Let All Mortal Flesh Keep Silence

Liturgy of St. James         8.7.8.7.8.7
Greek (4th cent.)
Trans. Gerard Moultrie (1864)

Let all mortal flesh keep silence,
And with fear and trembling stand;
Ponder nothing earthly-minded,
For with blessing in his hand,
Christ our God to earth descendeth,
Our full homage to demand.

King of kings, yet born of Mary,
As of old on earth he stood,
Lord of lords, in human vesture,
In the body and the blood,
He will give to all the faithful
His own self for heavenly food.

Rank on rank the host of heaven
Spreads its vanguard on the way,
As the Light of Light descendeth
From the realms of endless day,
That the powers of hell may vanish
As the darkness clears away.

At his feet the six-winged seraph;
Cherubim, with sleepless eye,
Veil their faces to the presence,
As with ceaseless voice they cry,
Alleluia, Alleluia,
Alleluia, Lord Most High!

## I Come with Joy

Brian Wren (1968, 1977) 8.6.8.6

I come with joy to meet my Lord,
Forgiven, loved, and free,
In awe and wonder to recall
His life laid down for me.

I come with Christians far and near
To find, as all are fed,
The new community of love
In Christ's communion bread.

As Christ breaks bread and bids us share,
Each proud division ends.
The love that made us, makes us one,
And strangers now are friends.

And thus with joy we meet our Lord.
His presence, always near,
Is in such friendship better known:
We see and praise him here.

Together met, together bound,
We'll go our different ways,
And as his people in the world,
We'll live and speak his praise.

# You Satisfy the Hungry Heart

Omer Westendorf (1976)                                    CM Refrain

You satisfy the hungry heart with gift of finest wheat;
Come give to us, O saving Lord, the bread of life to eat.

As when the shepherd calls his sheep,
They know and heed his voice;
So when you call your family, Lord,
We follow and rejoice.

With joyful lips we sing to you
Our praise and gratitude
That you should count us worthy, Lord,
To share this heavenly food.

Is not the cup we bless and share
The blood of Christ outpoured?
Do not one cup, one loaf, declare
Our oneness in the Lord?

The mystery of your presence, Lord,
No mortal tongue can tell:
Whom all the world cannot contain
Comes in our hearts to dwell.

You give yourself to us, O Lord;
Then selfless let us be,
To serve each other in your name
In truth and charity.

You satisfy the hungry heart with gift of finest wheat;
Come give to us, O saving Lord, the bread of life to eat.

## Bread of the World in Mercy Broken

Reginald Heber (publ. 1827)                                          9.8.9.8 D

Bread of the world in mercy broken,
Wine of the soul in mercy shed,
By whom the words of life were spoken,
And in whose death our sins are dead:
Look on the heart by sorrow broken,
Look on the tears by sinners shed;
And be thy feast to us the token
That by thy grace our souls are fed.

# Lord, Who the Night You Were Betrayed

William H. Turton (1881)                           10.10.10.10.10.10
                                                   John 17

Lord, who the night you were betrayed did pray
That all your church might be forever one:
Help us at every Eucharist to say
With willing heart and soul, "Your will be done."
That we may all one bread, one body be
Through this, your sacrament of unity.

For all your church on earth, we intercede;
Lord, make our sad divisions soon to cease;
Draw us all closer, each to each, we plead,
By drawing all to you, O Prince of Peace;
So may we all one bread, one body be,
Through this blest sacrament of unity.

And hear our prayer for wanderers from your fold;
Restore them, too, Good Shepherd of the sheep,
Back to the faith your saints confessed of old,
And to the church still pledged that faith to keep.
Soon may we all one bread, one body be,
Through this blest sacrament of unity.

So, Lord, at length when sacraments shall cease,
May we be one with all your church above—
One with your saints in one unbroken peace,
One as your bride in one unbounded love;
More blessed still, in peace and love to be
One with the Trinity in unity.

# Jesus, Thou Joy of Loving Hearts

Attr. Bernard of Clairvaux (12th cent.) LM
Trans. Ray Palmer (1858)

Jesus, thou joy of loving hearts,
Thou fount of life, thou light of all,
From the best bliss that earth imparts
We turn, unfilled, to heed thy call.

Thy truth unchanged hath ever stood;
Thou savest those that on thee call;
To them that seek thee thou art good,
To them that find thee, all in all.

We taste thee, O thou living bread,
And long to feast upon thee still;
We drink of thee, the fountainhead,
And thirst our souls from thee to fill.

Our restless spirits yearn for thee,
Where'er our changeful lot is cast,
Glad when thy gracious smile we see,
Blest when our faith can hold thee fast.

O Jesus, ever with us stay,
Make all our moments calm and bright;
O chase the night of sin away,
Shed o'er the world thy holy light.

# Here, O My Lord, I See Thee Face to Face

Horatius Bonar (1855)                                          10.10.10.10

Here, O my Lord, I see thee face to face;
Here would I touch and handle things unseen,
Here grasp with firmer hand the eternal grace,
And all my weariness upon thee lean.

Here would I feed upon the bread of God,
Here drink with thee the royal wine of heaven;
Here would I lay aside each earthly load,
Here taste afresh the calm of sin forgiven.

This is the hour of banquet and of song;
This is the heavenly table spread for me;
Here let me feast, and, feasting, still prolong
The brief, bright hour of fellowship with thee.

Too soon we rise; the symbols disappear;
The feast, though not the love, is past and gone;
The bread and wine remove, but Thou art here,
Nearer than ever, still my shield and sun.

I have no help but thine; nor do I need
Another arm save thine to lean upon;
It is enough, my Lord, enough indeed;
My strength is in thy might, thy might alone.

Mine is the sin, but thine the righteousness;
Mine is the guilt, but thine the cleansing blood;
Here is my robe, my refuge, and my peace—
Thy blood, thy righteousness, O Lord my God.

Feast after feast thus comes and passes by,
Yet, passing, points to the glad feast above,
Giving sweet foretaste of the festal joy,
The Lamb's great bridal feast of bliss and love.

## Be Known to Us in Breaking Bread

James Montgomery (1825) CM

Be known to us in breaking bread,
But do not then depart;
Savior, abide with us, and spread
Thy table in our heart.

There sup with us in love divine;
Thy body and thy blood,
That living bread, that heavenly wine,
Be our immortal food.

# Now the Silence

Jaroslav J. Vajda (1968)

Now the silence
Now the peace
Now the empty hands uplifted
Now the kneeling
Now the plea
Now the Father's arms in welcome
Now the hearing
Now the power
Now the vessel brimmed for pouring
Now the body
Now the blood
Now the joyful celebration
Now the wedding
Now the songs
Now the heart forgiven leaping
Now the Spirit's visitation
Now the Son's epiphany
Now the Father's blessing
Now
Now
Now

# Out of the Depths I Cry to Thee

Martin Luther (1524)                                    8.7.8.7.8.8.7
Trans. Edward Traill Horn III (1958)                    Psalm 130

Out of the depths I cry to thee,
O Lord, my sins bewailing!
Bow down thy gracious ear to me,
Make thou my prayer availing.
Mark not my misdeeds in thy book,
But on my sins in mercy look,
Or who can stand before thee?

With thee there is forgiveness, Lord,
And love and grace abounding;
The noblest thought and deed and word
Were else but empty sounding.
All guilty in thy sight appear;
All to thy presence come in fear,
And find thy lovingkindness.

Like those who watch upon the wall
To welcome in the morning,
My soul doth wait thy quiet call,
Herself with hope adorning.
So may all Israel look for thee,
And in thy day find mercy free,
And plenteous redemption.

# My Faith Looks Up to Thee

Ray Palmer (1830)                                                   6.6.4.6.6.6.4

My faith looks up to thee,
Thou Lamb of Calvary,
Savior divine:
Now hear me while I pray,
Take all my guilt away,
O let me from this day
Be wholly thine!

May thy rich grace impart
Strength to my fainting heart,
My zeal inspire;
As thou hast died for me,
O may my love to thee
Pure, warm, and changeless be,
A living fire!

While life's dark maze I tread,
And griefs around me spread,
Be thou my guide;
Bid darkness turn to day,
Wipe sorrow's tears away,
Nor let me ever stray
From thee aside.

When ends life's transient dream,
When death's cold, sullen stream
Shall o'er me roll,
Blest Savior, then, in love,
Fear and distrust remove;
O bear me safe above,
A ransomed soul!

# When in the Hour of Deepest Need

Paul Eber (c. 1560)                                               LM
Trans. Catherine Winkworth (1858)

When in the hour of deepest need
We know not where to look for aid;
When days and nights of anxious thought
No help or counsel yet have brought;

Our comfort then is this alone:
That we may meet before your throne
And cry to you, O faithful God,
For rescue from our sorry lot.

For you have made a promise true
To pardon those who flee to you,
Through him whose name alone is great,
Our Savior and our advocate.

And so we come, O God, today,
And all our woes before you lay;
For sorely tried, cast down, we stand,
Perplexed by fears on every hand.

Oh, from our sins hide not your face;
Absolve us through your boundless grace!
Be with us in our anguish still!
Free us at last from every ill!

So we with all our hearts each day
To you our glad thanksgiving pay,
Then walk obedient to your Word,
And now and ever praise you, Lord.

# And Can It Be That I Should Gain

Charles Wesley (1739)                                          8.8.8.8.8.8

And can it be that I should gain
An interest in the Savior's blood!
Died he for me? who caused his pain!
For me? who him to death pursued?
Amazing love! How can it be
That thou, my God, shouldst die for me?

'Tis mystery all: the Immortal dies!
Who can explore his strange design?
In vain the firstborn seraph tries
To sound the depths of love divine.
'Tis mercy all! Let earth adore;
Let angel minds inquire no more.

He left his Father's throne above
(So free, so infinite his grace!),
Emptied himself of all but love,
And bled for Adam's helpless race.
'Tis mercy all, immense and free,
For O my God, it found out me!

Long my imprisoned spirit lay,
Fast bound in sin and nature's night;
Thine eye diffused a quickening ray;
I woke, the dungeon flamed with light;
My chains fell off, my heart was free,
I rose, went forth, and followed thee.

No condemnation now I dread,
Jesus, and all in him, is mine;
Alive in him, my living Head,
And clothed in righteousness divine,
Bold I approach the eternal throne,
And claim the crown, through Christ my own.

## Blessed Assurance, Jesus Is Mine!

Fanny J. Crosby (1873) 9.10.9.9 Refrain

Blessed assurance, Jesus is mine!
O what a foretaste of glory divine!
Heir of salvation, purchase of God,
Born of his Spirit, washed in his blood.

Perfect submission, perfect delight,
Visions of rapture now burst on my sight;
Angels, descending, bring from above
Echoes of mercy, whispers of love.

Perfect submission, all is at rest,
I in my Savior am happy and blest,
Watching and waiting, looking above,
Filled with his goodness, lost in his love.

This is my story, this is my song,
Praising my Savior all the day long.

# Amazing Grace, How Sweet the Sound

Sts. 1–4, John Newton (1779)                                              CM
St. 5, *A Collection of Sacred Ballads* (1790)

Amazing grace, how sweet the sound,
That saved a wretch like me!
I once was lost, but now am found,
Was blind, but now I see.

'Twas grace that taught my heart to fear,
And grace my fears relieved;
How precious did that grace appear
The hour I first believed!

Through many dangers, toils, and snares,
I have already come;
'Tis grace has brought me safe thus far,
And grace will lead me home.

The Lord has promised good to me,
His word my hope secures;
He will my shield and portion be
As long as life endures.

When we've been there ten thousand years,
Bright shining as the sun,
We've no less days to sing God's praise
Than when we'd first begun.

# Come, Thou Fount of Every Blessing

Robert Robinson (c. 1758)                    8.7.8.7 D

Come, thou Fount of every blessing,
Tune my heart to sing thy grace;
Streams of mercy, never ceasing,
Call for songs of loudest praise.
Teach me some melodious sonnet,
Sung by flaming tongues above;
Praise the mount! I'm fixed upon it,
Mount of God's unchanging love!

Here I raise my Ebenezer,
Hither by thy help I'm come;
And I hope, by thy good pleasure,
Safely to arrive at home.
Jesus sought me when a stranger,
Wandering from the fold of God;
He, to rescue me from danger,
Interposed his precious blood.

O to grace how great a debtor
Daily I'm constrained to be!
Let that grace now, like a fetter,
Bind my wandering heart to thee:
Prone to wander, Lord, I feel it,
Prone to leave the God I love;
Here's my heart, O take and seal it,
Seal it for thy courts above.

## Lord Jesus, Think on Me

Synesius of Cyrene (early 5th cent.)       SM
Trans. Allen W. Chatfield (1876)

Lord Jesus, think on me,
And purge away my sin;
From earth-born passions set me free,
And make me pure within.

Lord Jesus, think on me,
Amid the battle's strife;
In all my pain and misery
Be thou my health and life.

Lord Jesus, think on me,
Nor let me go astray;
Through darkness and perplexity
Point thou the heavenly way.

Lord Jesus, think on me,
That, when this life is past,
I may the eternal brightness see,
And share thy joy at last.

# Once He Came in Blessing

Johann Horn (1544)
Trans. Catherine Winkworth (1863)

8.6.8.6.8.6

Once he came in blessing,
All our ills redressing;
Came in likeness lowly,
Son of God most holy;
Bore the cross to save us;
Hope and freedom gave us.

Still he comes within us;
Still his voice would win us
From the sins that hurt us;
Would to truth convert us
From our foolish error
Ere he comes in terror.

Thus, if you have known him,
Not ashamed to own him,
Nor have spurned him coldly,
But will trust him boldly,
He will then receive you,
Heal you, and forgive you.

Those who then are loyal
Find a welcome royal.
Come, then, O Lord Jesus,
From our sins release us;
Let us here confess you,
Till in heaven we bless you.

# O Christ, Our Hope

Latin (8th cent.)                                      8.6.8.6
Trans. John Chandler (1837)

O Christ, our hope, our hearts' desire,
Creation's mighty Lord,
Redeemer of the fallen world,
By holy love outpoured.

How vast your mercy to accept
The burden of our sin,
And bow your head in cruel death
To make us clean within.

But now the bonds of death are burst,
The ransom has been paid;
You now ascend the Father's throne
In robes of light arrayed.

Oh, let your mighty love prevail
To purge us of our pride,
That we may stand before your throne
By mercy purified.

Christ Jesus, be our present joy,
Our future great reward;
Our only glory, may it be
To glory in the Lord!

All praise to you, ascended Lord;
All glory ever be
To Father, Son, and Holy Ghost
Through all eternity!

# There Is a Balm in Gilead

African-American spiritual (19th cent.)

There is a balm in Gilead to make the wounded whole.
There is a balm in Gilead to heal the sin-sick soul.

Sometimes I feel discouraged,
And think my work's in vain,
But then the Holy Spirit
Revives my soul again.

Don't ever feel discouraged,
For Jesus is your friend,
And if you lack for knowledge
He'll not refuse to lend.

If you cannot preach like Peter,
If you cannot pray like Paul,
You can tell the love of Jesus
And say, "He died for all."

There is a balm in Gilead to make the wounded whole.
There is a balm in Gilead to heal the sin-sick soul.

## There's a Wideness in God's Mercy

Frederick William Faber (1854)                                    8.7.8.7 D

There's a wideness in God's mercy
Like the wideness of the sea;
There's a kindness in his justice,
Which is more than liberty.
There is welcome for the sinner,
And more graces for the good;
There is mercy with the Savior;
There is healing in his blood.

There is no place where earth's sorrows
Are more felt than up in heaven;
There is no place where earth's failings
Have such kindly judgment given.
There is plentiful redemption
In the blood that has been shed;
There is joy for all the members
In the sorrows of the Head.

For the love of God is broader
Than the measure of the mind;
And the heart of the Eternal
Is most wonderfully kind.
If our love were but more simple,
We should take him at his word;
And our lives would be all sunshine
In the sweetness of the Lord.

# Your Heart, O God, Is Grieved

*Kyrie,* trope
Jiři Tranovský (1636)
Trans. Jaroslav J. Vajda (1962)

O God, Father in heaven, have mercy upon us.
  Your heart, O God, is grieved, we know,
  By every evil, every woe;
  Upon your cross-forsaken Son
  Our death is laid, and peace is won.

O Son of God, redeemer of the world, have mercy
      upon us.
  Your arms extend, O Christ, to save
  From sting of death and grasp of grave;
  Your scars before the Father move
  His heart to mercy at such love.

O God, Holy Spirit, have mercy upon us.
  O lavish Giver, come to aid
  The feeble child your grace has made.
  Now make us grow and help us pray;
  Bring joy and comfort; come to stay.

## Who Is on the Lord's Side?

Frances Ridley Havergal (1877)                    6.5.6.5.6.5 D

Who is on the Lord's side?
Who will serve the King?
Who will be his helpers,
Other lives to bring?
Who will leave the world's side?
Who will face the foe?
Who is on the Lord's side?
Who for him will go?
By thy call of mercy,
By thy grace divine,
We are on the Lord's side,
Savior, we are thine.

Not for weight of glory,
Not for crown and palm,
Enter we the army,
Raise the warrior psalm;
But for Love that claimeth
Lives for whom he died:
All whom Jesus nameth
Must be on his side.
By thy love constraining,
By thy grace divine,
We are on the Lord's side,
Savior, we are thine.

Jesus, thou hast bought us,
Not with gold or gem,
But with thine own lifeblood,
For thy diadem:
With thy blessing filling
Each who comes to thee,
Thou hast made us willing,
Thou hast made us free.
By thy grand redemption,
By thy grace divine,
We are on the Lord's side,
Savior, we are thine.

## I Sought the Lord

Anon. U.S.A. (1880)                                    10.10.10.6

I sought the Lord, and afterward I knew
He moved my soul to seek him, seeking me.
It was not I that found, O Savior true;
No, I was found of thee.

Thou didst reach forth thy hand and mine enfold;
I walked and sank not on the storm-vexed sea.
'Twas not so much that I on thee took hold,
As thou, dear Lord, on me.

I find, I walk, I love, but oh, the whole
Of love is but my answer, Lord, to thee!
For thou wert long beforehand with my soul;
Always thou lovedst me.

# Abide with Us, Our Savior

Josua Stegmann (1628)　　　　　　　　　　7.6.7.6
Trans. composite

Abide with us, our Savior,
Nor let your mercy cease;
From Satan's might defend us,
And grant our souls release.

Abide with us, our Savior,
Sustain us by your Word;
That we with all your people
To life may be restored.

Abide among us always,
Lord, with your faithfulness;
O Jesus, leave us never,
But help us in distress.

Abide with us, our Savior,
O Light of endless light,
Bestow on us your blessings,
And save us by your might.

# Dear Lord and Father of Mankind

John Greenleaf Whittier (1872)                    8.6.8.8.6

Dear Lord and Father of mankind,
Forgive our foolish ways;
Reclothe us in our rightful mind,
In purer lives thy service find,
In deeper reverence, praise.

In simple trust like theirs who heard,
Beside the Syrian sea,
The gracious calling of the Lord,
Let us, like them, without a word
Rise up and follow thee.

O Sabbath rest by Galilee,
O calm of hills above,
Where Jesus knelt to share with thee
The silence of eternity,
Interpreted by love!

Drop thy still dews of quietness,
Till all our strivings cease;
Take from our souls the strain and stress,
And let our ordered lives confess
The beauty of thy peace.

Breathe through the heats of our desire
Thy coolness and thy balm;
Let sense be dumb, let flesh retire;
Speak through the earthquake, wind, and fire,
O still, small voice of calm!

## Great God, Your Love Has Called Us Here

Brian Wren (1973) 8.8.8.8.8.8

Great God, your love has called us here
As we, by love, for love were made.
Your living likeness still we bear,
Though marred, dishonored, disobeyed.
We come, with all our heart and mind
Your call to hear, your love to find.

We come with self-inflicted pains
Of broken trust and chosen wrong,
Half-free, half-bound by inner chains,
By social forces swept along,
By powers and systems close confined
Yet seeking hope for humankind.

Great God, in Christ you call our name
And then receive us as your own,
Not through some merit, right, or claim
But by your gracious love alone.
We strain to glimpse your mercy seat
And find you kneeling at our feet.

Then take the towel, and break the bread,
And humble us, and call us friends.
Suffer and serve till all are fed,
And show how grandly love intends
To work till all creation sings,
To fill all worlds, to crown all things.

Great God, in Christ you set us free
Your life to live, your joy to share.
Give us your Spirit's liberty
To turn from guilt and dull despair,
And offer all that faith can do
While love is making all things new.


## Eternal Ruler of the Ceaseless Round

John White Chadwick (1864)                    10.10.10.10.10.10

Eternal Ruler of the ceaseless round
Of circling planets singing on their way,
Guide of the nations from the night profound
Into the glory of the perfect day;
Rule in our hearts, that we may ever be
Guided and strengthened and upheld by thee.

We would be one in hatred of all wrong,
One in the love of all things sweet and fair,
One with the joy that breaketh into song,
One with the grief that trembleth into prayer;
One in the power that makes thy children free
To follow truth, and thus to follow thee.

Oh, clothe us with thy heavenly armor, Lord,
Thy trusty shield, thy sword of love divine;
Our inspiration be thy constant word,
We ask no victories that are not thine;
Give or withhold, let pain or pleasure be;
Enough to know that we are serving thee.

# How Firm a Foundation

"K" in Rippon's *Selection of Hymns* (1787)                11.11.11.11
Isaiah 43:1–2

How firm a foundation, ye saints of the Lord,
Is laid for your faith in his excellent word!
What more can he say than to you he hath said,
To you who for refuge to Jesus have fled?

"Fear not, I am with thee, O be not dismayed,
For I am thy God and will still give thee aid;
I'll strengthen and help thee, and cause thee to stand,
Upheld by my righteous, omnipotent hand.

"When through the deep waters I call thee to go,
The rivers of woe shall not thee overflow;
For I will be with thee, thy troubles to bless,
And sanctify to thee thy deepest distress.

"When through fiery trials thy pathways shall lie,
My grace, all sufficient, shall be thy supply;
The flame shall not hurt thee; I only design
Thy dross to consume, and thy gold to refine.

"E'en down to old age all my people shall prove
My sovereign, eternal, unchangeable love;
And when hoary hairs shall their temples adorn,
Like lambs they shall still in my bosom be borne.

"The soul that on Jesus still leans for repose,
I will not, I will not desert to its foes;
That soul, though all hell should endeavor to shake,
I'll never, no, never, no, never forsake."

# Jesus, Thy Boundless Love to Me

Paul Gerhardt (1653) 8.8.8.8.8.8
Trans. John Wesley (1739)

Jesus, thy boundless love to me
No thought can reach, no tongue declare;
O knit my thankful heart to thee,
And reign without a rival there!
Thine wholly, thine alone, I'd live,
Myself to thee entirely give.

O grant that nothing in my soul
May dwell, but thy pure love alone;
O may thy love possess me whole,
My joy, my treasure, and my crown!
All coldness from my heart remove;
May every act, word, thought be love.

O Love, how gracious is thy way!
All fear before thy presence flies;
Care, anguish, sorrow melt away,
Where'er thy healing beams arise.
O Jesus, nothing may I see,
Nothing desire, or seek, but thee.

## Trust and Obey

John H. Sammis (1887)　　　　　　　　　　　　　6.6.9 D Refrain

When we walk with the Lord
In the light of his word,
What a glory he sheds on our way!
While we do his good will,
He abides with us still,
And with all who will trust and obey.

Not a burden we bear,
Not a sorrow we share,
But our toil he doth richly repay;
Not a grief or a loss,
Not a frown or a cross,
But is blest if we trust and obey.

But we never can prove
The delights of his love
Until all on the altar we lay;
For the favor he shows,
For the joy he bestows,
Are for them who will trust and obey.

Then in fellowship sweet
We will sit at his feet,
Or we'll walk by his side in the way;
What he says we will do,
Where he sends we will go;
Never fear, only trust and obey.

Trust and obey,
For there's no other way
To be happy in Jesus,
But to trust and obey.

# Come, My Way, My Truth, My Life

George Herbert (publ. 1633)                                     7.7.7.7
                                                              John 14:6

Come, my Way, my Truth, my Life:
Such a way as gives us breath;
Such a truth as ends all strife;
Such a life as killeth death.

Come, my Light, my Feast, my Strength:
Such a light as shows a feast;
Such a feast as mends in length;
Such a strength as makes his guest.

Come, my Joy, my Love, my Heart:
Such a joy as none can move;
Such a love as none can part;
Such a heart as joys in love.

## Love Divine, All Loves Excelling

Charles Wesley (1747)                                    8.7.8.7 D

Love divine, all loves excelling,
Joy of heaven, to earth come down,
Fix in us thy humble dwelling,
All thy faithful mercies crown!
Jesus, thou art all compassion,
Pure, unbounded love thou art;
Visit us with thy salvation,
Enter every trembling heart.

Breathe, O breathe thy loving Spirit
Into every troubled breast!
Let us all in thee inherit,
Let us find the promised rest;
Take away the love of sinning;
Alpha and Omega be;
End of faith, as its beginning,
Set our hearts at liberty.

Come, Almighty to deliver,
Let us all thy life receive;
Suddenly return, and never,
Nevermore thy temples leave.
Thee we would be always blessing,
Serve thee as thy hosts above;
Pray, and praise thee without ceasing,
Glory in thy perfect love.

Finish, then, thy new creation;
Pure and spotless let us be;
Let us see thy great salvation
Perfectly restored in thee;

Changed from glory into glory,
Till in heaven we take our place,
Till we cast our crowns before thee,
Lost in wonder, love, and praise.

## Just as I Am, without One Plea

Charlotte Elliott (1834)                                                    LM

Just as I am, without one plea
But that thy blood was shed for me,
And that thou bidd'st me come to thee,
O Lamb of God, I come, I come!

Just as I am, though tossed about
With many a conflict, many a doubt,
Fightings and fears within, without,
O Lamb of God, I come, I come!

Just as I am, thou wilt receive,
Wilt welcome, pardon, cleanse, relieve;
Because thy promise I believe,
O Lamb of God, I come, I come!

Just as I am, thy love unknown
Has broken every barrier down;
Now to be thine, yea, thine alone,
O Lamb of God, I come, I come!

# Make Me a Captive, Lord

George Matheson (1890)                                                    SM

Make me a captive, Lord,
And then I shall be free;
Force me to render up my sword,
And I shall conqueror be.

I sink in life's alarms
When by myself I stand;
Imprison me within thine arms,
And strong shall be my hand.

My heart is weak and poor
Until it master find;
It has no spring of action sure.
It varies with the wind.

It cannot freely move
Till thou hast wrought its chain;
Enslave it with thy matchless love,
And deathless it shall reign.

My will is not my own
Till thou hast made it thine;
If it would reach a monarch's throne,
It must its crown resign;

It only stands unbent
Amid the clashing strife,
When on thy bosom it has leant,
And found in thee its life.

# May the Mind of Christ My Savior

Kate B. Wilkinson (1925)                                                    8.7.8.5

May the mind of Christ my Savior
Live in me from day to day,
By his love and power controlling
All I do and say.

May the Word of God dwell richly
In my heart from hour to hour,
So that all may see I triumph
Only through his power.

May the peace of God my Father
Rule my life in everything,
That I may be calm to comfort
Sick and sorrowing.

May the love of Jesus fill me
As the waters fill the sea,
Him exalting, self abasing—
This is victory.

May I run the race before me,
Strong and brave to face the foe,
Looking only unto Jesus
As I onward go.

May his beauty rest upon me
As I seek the lost to win,
And may they forget the channel,
Seeing only him.

# O for a Closer Walk with God

William Cowper (1769)                                    CM

O for a closer walk with God,
A calm and heavenly frame,
A light to shine upon the road
That leads me to the Lamb!

Where is the blessedness I knew
When first I saw the Lord?
Where is the soul-refreshing view
Of Jesus and his word?

Return, O holy Dove, return,
Sweet messenger of rest;
I hate the sins that made thee mourn,
And drove thee from my breast.

The dearest idol I have known,
Whate'er that idol be,
Help me to tear it from thy throne,
And worship only thee.

So shall my walk be close with God,
Calm and serene my frame;
So purer light shall mark the road
That leads me to the Lamb.

# Be Thou My Vision

Irish (c. 700)                                    10.10.9.10
Trans. Mary E. Byrne (1905)
Vers. Eleanor Hull (1912)

Be thou my vision, O Lord of my heart;
Nought be all else to me, save that thou art—
Thou my best thought, by day or by night,
Waking or sleeping, thy presence my light.

Be thou my wisdom, and thou my true word;
I ever with thee and thou with me, Lord;
Heart of my own heart, whatever befall,
Still be my vision, O Ruler of all.

Riches I heed not, nor vain, empty praise,
Thou mine inheritance, now and always:
Thou and thou only, first in my heart,
Great God of Heaven, my treasure thou art.

High King of heaven, my victory won,
May I reach heaven's joys, O bright heaven's Sun!
Heart of my own heart, whatever befall,
Still be my vision, O Ruler of all.

# O Savior, in This Quiet Place

Fred Pratt Green (1974)                                                    CM

O Savior, in this quiet place,
Where anyone may kneel,
I also come to ask for grace,
Believing you can heal.

If pain of body, stress of mind,
Destroys my inward peace,
In prayer for others may I find
The secret of release.

If self upon its sickness feeds
And turns my life to gall,
Let me not brood upon my needs,
But simply tell you all.

You never said, "You ask too much,"
To any troubled soul.
I long to feel your healing touch;
Will you not make me whole?

But if the thing I most desire
Is not your way for me,
May faith, when tested in the fire,
Prove its integrity.

Of all my prayers, may this be chief:
Till faith is fully grown,
Lord, disbelieve my unbelief,
And claim me as your own.

# Prayer Is the Soul's Sincere Desire

James Montgomery (1818)                                              CM

Prayer is the soul's sincere desire,
Unuttered or expressed,
The motion of a hidden fire
That trembles in the breast.

Prayer is the burden of a sigh,
The falling of a tear,
The upward glancing of an eye,
When none but God is near.

Prayer is the simplest form of speech
That infant lips can try;
Prayer the sublimest strains that reach
The Majesty on high.

Prayer is the contrite sinners' voice,
Returning from their way,
While angels in their songs rejoice
And cry, "Behold, they pray!"

# Take My Life

Frances Ridley Havergal (1874)                    7.7.7.7

Take my life, and let it be
Consecrated, Lord, to thee.
Take my moments and my days;
Let them flow in ceaseless praise.

Take my hands, and let them move
At the impulse of thy love.
Take my feet, and let them be
Swift and beautiful for thee.

Take my voice, and let me sing,
Always, only, for my King.
Take my lips, and let them be
Filled with messages from thee.

Take my silver and my gold,
Not a mite would I withhold;
Take my intellect, and use
Every power as thou shalt choose.

Take my will, and make it thine;
It shall be no longer mine.
Take my heart, it is thine own;
It shall be thy royal throne.

Take my love; my Lord, I pour
At thy feet its treasure store.
Take myself, and I will be
Ever, only, all for thee.

# What a Friend We Have in Jesus

Joseph Scriven (1855)

8.7.8.7 D

What a friend we have in Jesus,
All our sins and griefs to bear!
What a privilege to carry
Everything to God in prayer!
O what peace we often forfeit,
O what needless pain we bear,
All because we do not carry
Everything to God in prayer!

Have we trials and temptations?
Is there trouble anywhere?
We should never be discouraged:
Take it to the Lord in prayer!
Can we find a friend so faithful,
Who will all our sorrows share?
Jesus knows our every weakness;
Take it to the Lord in prayer!

Are we weak and heavy laden,
Cumbered with a load of care?
Precious Savior, still our refuge—
Take it to the Lord in prayer!
Do thy friends despise, forsake thee?
Take it to the Lord in prayer!
In his arms he'll take and shield thee,
Thou wilt find a solace there.

# Seek the Lord

Fred Pratt Green (1986)                                          8.7.8.7 D
                                                                Isaiah 55:6–11

Seek the Lord who now is present,
Pray to One who is at hand.
Let the wicked cease from sinning,
Evildoers change their mind.
On the sinful God has pity;
Those returning God forgives.
This is what the Lord is saying
To a world that disbelieves.

"Judge me not by human standards!
As the vault of heaven soars
High above the earth, so higher
Are my thoughts and ways than yours.
See how rain and snow from heaven
Make earth blossom and bear fruit,
Giving you, before returning,
Seed for sowing, bread to eat:

"So my word returns not fruitless;
Does not from its labors cease
Till it has achieved my purpose
In a world of joy and peace."
God is love! How close the prophet
To that vital gospel word!
In Isaiah's inspiration
It is Jesus we have heard!

# All Who Would Valiant Be

John Bunyan (1684), adapted                6.5.6.5.6.6.6.5

All who would valiant be
'Gainst all disaster,
Let them in constancy
Follow the Master.
There's no discouragement
Shall make them once relent
Their first avowed intent
To be true pilgrims.

Who so beset them round
With dismal stories,
Do but themselves confound;
Their strength the more is.
No foes shall stay their might;
Though they with giants fight,
They will make good their right
To be true pilgrims.

Since, Lord, you will defend
Us with your Spirit,
We know we at the end
Shall life inherit.
Then fancies flee away!
We'll fear not what they say,
We'll labor night and day
To be true pilgrims.

# As Saints of Old Their Firstfruits Brought

Frank von Christierson (1960)             CMD

As saints of old their firstfruits brought
Of orchard, flock, and field
To God, the giver of all good,
The source of bounteous yield;
So we today firstfruits would bring:
The wealth of this good land,
Of farm and market, shop and home,
Of mind and heart and hand.

A world in need now summons us
To labor, love, and give;
To make our life an offering
That others too may live.
The church of Christ is calling us
To keep this end in view:
A world redeemed, your kingdom come,
All life in Christ made new.

In gratitude and humble trust
We bring our best today
To serve your cause and share your love
With all along life's way.
O God, who gave yourself to us
In Jesus Christ, your Son,
Teach us to give ourselves each day
Until life's work is done.

# Forth in the Peace of Christ We Go

James Quinn (1969)

LM

Forth in the peace of Christ we go;
Christ to the world with joy we bring;
Christ in our minds, Christ on our lips,
Christ in our hearts, the world's true King.

King of our hearts, Christ makes us kings;
Kingship with him his servants gain;
With Christ, the Servant Lord of all,
Christ's world we serve to share Christ's reign.

Priests of the world, Christ sends us forth
The world of time to consecrate,
The world of sin by grace to heal,
Christ's world in Christ to recreate.

Christ's are our lips, his word we speak;
Prophets are we whose deeds proclaim
Christ's truth in love that we may be
Christ in the world, to spread Christ's name.

We are the church: Christ bids us show
That in his church all nations find
Their hearth and home, where Christ restores
True peace, true love, to all mankind.

# God of Grace and God of Glory

Harry Emerson Fosdick (1930)                              8.7.8.7.8.7

God of grace and God of glory,
On thy people pour Thy power;
Crown thine ancient church's story;
Bring its bud to glorious flower.
Grant us wisdom, grant us courage,
For the facing of this hour.

Lo! the hosts of evil round us
Scorn thy Christ, assail thy ways!
From the fears that long have bound us
Free our hearts to faith and praise.
Grant us wisdom, grant us courage,
For the living of these days.

Cure thy children's warring madness,
Bend our pride to thy control;
Shame our wanton, selfish gladness,
Rich in things and poor in soul.
Grant us wisdom, grant us courage,
Lest we miss thy kingdom's goal.

Set our feet on lofty places;
Gird our lives that they may be
Armored with all Christlike graces,
Pledged to set all captives free.
Grant us wisdom, grant us courage,
That we fail not them nor thee!

Save us from weak resignation
To the evils we deplore;
Let the gift of thy salvation
Be our glory evermore.
Grant us wisdom, grant us courage,
Serving thee whom we adore.


# O Master, Let Me Walk with Thee

Washington Gladden (1879)                                    LM

O Master, let me walk with thee
In lowly paths of service free;
Tell me thy secret; help me bear
The strain of toil, the fret of care.

Help me the slow of heart to move
By some clear, winning word of love;
Teach me the wayward feet to stay,
And guide them in the homeward way.

Teach me thy patience; still with thee
In closer, dearer company,
In work that keeps faith sweet and strong,
In trust that triumphs over wrong.

In hope that sends a shining ray
Far down the future's broadening way;
In peace that only thou canst give,
With thee, O Master, let me live.

# God the Spirit, Guide and Guardian

Carl P. Daw, Jr. (1988)                                    8.7.8.7 D

God the Spirit, guide and guardian,
Wind-sped flame and hovering dove,
Breath of life and voice of prophets,
Sign of blessing, power of love:
Give to those who lead your people
Fresh anointing of your grace;
Send them forth as bold apostles
To your church in every place.

Christ our Savior, Sovereign, Shepherd,
Word made flesh, Love crucified,
Teacher, healer, suffering Servant,
Friend of sinners, foe of pride:
In your tending may all pastors
Learn and live a Shepherd's care;
Grant them courage and compassion
Shown through word and deed and prayer.

Great Creator, Life-bestower,
Truth beyond all thought's recall,
Fount of wisdom, womb of mercy,
Giving and forgiving all:
As you know our strength and weakness,
So may those the church exalts
Oversee her life steadfastly,
Yet not overlook her faults.

Triune God, mysterious Being,
Undivided and diverse,
Deeper than our minds can fathom,
Greater than our creeds rehearse:
Help us in our varied callings
Your full image to proclaim,
That our ministries uniting
May give glory to your name.

## O Christians, Haste

Mary A. Thomson (1868)                    11.10.11.10 Refrain

O Christians, haste, your mission high fulfilling,
To tell to all the world that God is Light;
That he who made all nations is not willing
One soul should perish, lost in shades of night.

Proclaim to every people, tongue, and nation
That God, in whom they live and move, is Love:
Tell how he stooped to save his lost creation,
And died on earth that we might live above.

Send heralds forth to bear the message glorious;
Give of your wealth to speed them on their way;
Pour out your soul for them in prayer victorious;
And all your spending Jesus will repay.

Publish glad tidings, tidings of peace,
Tidings of Jesus, redemption, and release.

# Hope of the World

Georgia Harkness (1954)                                              11.10.11.10

Hope of the world, thou Christ of great compassion,
Speak to our fearful hearts by conflict rent.
Save us, thy people, from consuming passion,
Who by our own false hopes and aims are spent.

Hope of the world, God's gift from highest heaven,
Bringing to hungry souls the bread of life,
Still let thy Spirit unto us be given
To heal earth's wounds and end our bitter strife.

Hope of the world, afoot on dusty highways,
Showing to wandering souls the path of light,
Walk thou beside us lest the tempting byways
Lure us away from thee to endless night.

Hope of the world, who by thy cross didst save us
From death and deep despair, from sin and guilt,
We render back the love thy mercy gave us;
Take thou our lives and use them as thou wilt.

Hope of the world, O Christ, o'er death victorious,
Who by this sign didst conquer grief and pain,
We would be faithful to thy gospel glorious:
Thou art our Lord! Thou dost forever reign!

# How Clear Is Our Vocation, Lord

Fred Pratt Green (1981)                                    8.6.8.8.6.6

How clear is our vocation, Lord,
When once we heed your call:
To live according to your word,
And daily learn, refreshed, restored,
That you are Lord of all
And will not let us fall.

But if, forgetful, we should find
Your yoke is hard to bear,
If worldly pressures fray the mind
And love itself cannot unwind
Its tangled skein of care:
Our inward life repair.

We mark your saints, how they became
In hindrances more sure,
Whose joyful virtues put to shame
The casual way we wear your name,
And by our faults obscure
Your power to cleanse and cure.

In what you give us, Lord, to do,
Together or alone,
In old routines or ventures new,
May we not cease to look to you—
The cross you hung upon—
All you endeavored done.

# Lead On, O King Eternal

Ernest W. Shurtleff (1888)                                    7.6.7.6 D

Lead on, O King eternal,
The day of march has come;
Henceforth in fields of conquest
Thy tents shall be our home:
Through days of preparation
Thy grace has made us strong,
And now, O King eternal,
We lift our battle song.

Lead on, O King eternal,
Till sin's fierce war shall cease,
And holiness shall whisper
The sweet amen of peace;
For not with swords' loud clashing,
Nor roll of stirring drums;
With deeds of love and mercy
The heavenly kingdom comes.

Lead on, O King eternal:
We follow, not with fears;
For gladness breaks like morning
Where'er thy face appears;
Thy cross is lifted o'er us;
We journey in its light:
The crown awaits the conquest;
Lead on, O God of might.

# O Day of God, Draw Nigh

Robert B. Y. Scott (1937)

SM

O day of God, draw nigh
In beauty and in power,
Come with your timeless judgment now
To match our present hour.

Bring to our troubled minds,
Uncertain and afraid,
The quiet of a steadfast faith,
Calm of a call obeyed.

Bring justice to our land,
That all may dwell secure,
And finely build for days to come
Foundations that endure.

Bring to our world of strife
Your sovereign word of peace,
That war may haunt the earth no more
And desolation cease.

O day of God, draw nigh
As at creation's birth;
Let there be light again, and set
Your judgments in the earth.

Used by permission of Emmanuel College, Toronto.

# Lord, You Give the Great Commission

Jeffery Rowthorn (1978)    8.7.8.7 D

Lord, you give the great commission:
"Heal the sick and preach the word."
Lest the church neglect its mission,
And the gospel go unheard,
Help us witness to your purpose
With renewed integrity;
    With the Spirit's gifts empower us
    For the work of ministry.

Lord, you call us to your service:
"In my name baptize and teach."
That the world may trust your promise,
Life abundant meant for each,
Give us all new fervor, draw us
Closer in community;
    With the Spirit's gifts empower us
    For the work of ministry.

Lord, you make the common holy:
"This my body, this my blood."
Let us all, for earth's true glory,
Daily lift life heavenward,
Asking that the world around us
Share your children's liberty;
    With the Spirit's gifts empower us
    For the work of ministry.

Lord, you show us love's true measure:
"Father, what they do, forgive."
Yet we hoard as private treasure
All that you so freely give.
May your care and mercy lead us
To a just society;
    With the Spirit's gifts empower us
    For the work of ministry.

Lord, you bless with words assuring:
"I am with you to the end."
Faith and hope and love restoring,
May we serve as you intend,
And, amid the cares that claim us,
Hold in mind eternity;
    With the Spirit's gifts empower us
    For the work of ministry.

# O God of Earth and Altar

Gilbert K. Chesterton (1906)                                    7.6.7.6 D

O God of earth and altar,
Bow down and hear our cry,
Our earthly rulers falter,
Our people drift and die;
The walls of gold entomb us,
The swords of scorn divide,
Take not thy thunder from us,
But take away our pride.

From all that terror teaches,
From lies of tongue and pen,
From all the easy speeches
That comfort cruel men,
From sale and profanation
Of honor, and the sword,
From sleep and from damnation,
Deliver us, good Lord!

Tie in a living tether
The prince and priest and thrall,
Bind all our lives together,
Smite us and save us all;
In ire and exultation
Aflame with faith, and free,
Lift up a living nation,
A single sword to thee.

# Lord, Whose Love through Humble Service

Albert F. Bayly (1961)                    8.7.8.7 D

Lord, whose love through humble service
Bore the weight of human need,
Who upon the cross, forsaken,
Offered mercy's perfect deed,
We, your servants, bring the worship
Not of voice alone, but heart,
Consecrating to your purpose
Every gift that you impart.

Still your children wander homeless;
Still the hungry cry for bread;
Still the captives long for freedom;
Still in grief we mourn our dead.
As, O Lord, your deep compassion
Healed the sick and freed the soul,
Use the love your Spirit kindles
Still to save and make us whole.

As we worship, grant us vision,
Till your love's revealing light,
In its height and depth and greatness,
Dawns upon our quickened sight,
Making known the needs and burdens
Your compassion bids us bear,
Stirring us to tireless striving,
Your abundant life to share.

(*continued*)

Called from worship to your service,
Forth in your dear name we go,
To the child, the youth, the aged,
Love in living deeds to show;
Hope and health, goodwill and comfort,
Counsel, aid, and peace we give,
That your servants, Lord, in freedom
May your mercy know and live.

## O God of Every Nation

William W. Reid, Jr. (1958)                     7.6.7.6 D

O God of every nation,
Of every race and land,
Redeem the whole creation
With your almighty hand;
Where hate and fear divide us
And bitter threats are hurled,
In love and mercy guide us
And heal our strife-torn world.

From search for wealth and power
And scorn of truth and right,
From trust in bombs that shower
Destruction through the night,
From pride of race and station
And blindness to your way,
Deliver every nation,
Eternal God, we pray.

Lord, strengthen those who labor
That all may find release
From fear of rattling saber,
From dread of war's increase;
When hope and courage falter,
Your still small voice be heard;
With faith that none can alter,
Your servants undergird.

Keep bright in us the vision
Of days when war shall cease,
When hatred and division
Give way to love and peace,
Till dawns the morning glorious
When peace on earth shall reign
And Christ shall rule victorious
O'er all the world's domain.

## Not for Tongues of Heaven's Angels

Timothy Dudley-Smith (1984)                    8.7.8.7.6
1 Corinthians 13

Not for tongues of heaven's angels,
Not for wisdom to discern,
Not for faith that masters mountains;
For this better gift we yearn:
May love be ours, O Lord.

Love is humble, love is gentle,
Love is tender, true, and kind;
Love is gracious, ever-patient,
Generous of heart and mind:
May love be ours, O Lord.

Never jealous, never selfish,
Love will not rejoice in wrong;
Never boastful nor resentful,
Love believes and suffers long:
May love be ours, O Lord.

In the day this world is fading
Faith and hope will play their part;
But when Christ is seen in glory
Love shall reign in every heart:
May love be ours, O Lord.

# O Jesus, I Have Promised

John Ernest Bode (1868)                              7.6.7.6 D

O Jesus, I have promised
To serve thee to the end;
Be thou forever near me,
My Master and my friend;
I shall not fear the battle
If thou art by my side,
Nor wander from the pathway
If thou wilt be my guide.

O let me feel thee near me!
The world is ever near;
I see the sights that dazzle,
The tempting sounds I hear;
My foes are ever near me,
Around me and within;
But, Jesus, draw thou nearer
And shield my soul from sin.

O let me hear thee speaking
In accents clear and still,
Above the storms of passion,
The murmurs of self-will;
O speak to reassure me,
To hasten or control;
O speak, and make me listen,
Thou guardian of my soul.

*(continued)*

O Jesus, thou hast promised
To all who follow thee
That where thou art in glory
There shall thy servant be;
And, Jesus, I have promised
To serve thee to the end;
O give me grace to follow,
My Master and my friend.

## Soldiers of Christ, Arise

Charles Wesley (1749)                                        SMD
                                             Ephesians 6:13–18

Soldiers of Christ, arise,
And put your armor on,
Strong in the strength which God supplies
Through his eternal Son;
Strong in the Lord of Hosts,
And in his mighty power,
Who in the strength of Jesus trusts
Is more than conqueror.

Stand then in his great might,
With all his strength endued,
But take to arm you for the fight
The panoply of God;
That having all things done,
And all your conflicts passed,
You may o'ercome through Christ alone
And stand entire at last.

Pray without ceasing, pray,
(Your Captain gives the word)
His summons cheerfully obey
And call upon the Lord;
To God your every want
In instant prayer display,
Pray always, pray and never faint,
Pray, without ceasing pray.

From strength to strength go on,
Wrestle and fight and pray,
Tread all the powers of darkness down
And win the well-fought day.
Still let the Spirit cry
In all his soldiers, "Come!"
Till Christ the Lord descends from high
And takes the conquerors home.

# There's a Spirit in the Air

Brian Wren (1969)  7.7.7.7

There's a spirit in the air,
Telling Christians everywhere:
"Praise the love that Christ revealed,
Living, working in our world."

Lose your shyness, find your tongue,
Tell the world what God has done:
God in Christ has come to stay.
Live tomorrow's life today!

When believers break the bread,
When a hungry child is fed,
Praise the love that Christ revealed,
Living, working in our world!

Still the Spirit gives us light,
Seeing wrong and setting right:
God in Christ has come to stay.
Live tomorrow's life today!

When a stranger's not alone,
Where the homeless find a home,
Praise the love that Christ revealed,
Living, working in our world.

May the Spirit fill our praise,
Guide our thoughts and change our ways.
God in Christ has come to stay.
Live tomorrow's life today!

There's a Spirit in the air,
Calling people everywhere;
Praise the love that Christ revealed,
Living, working in our world.

# Where Cross the Crowded Ways of Life

Frank Mason North (1905)                                        LM

Where cross the crowded ways of life,
Where sound the cries of race and clan,
Above the noise of selfish strife,
We hear thy voice, O Son of Man.

In haunts of wretchedness and need,
On shadowed thresholds fraught with fears,
From paths where hide the lures of greed,
We catch the vision of thy tears.

From tender childhood's helplessness,
From human grief and burdened toil,
From famished souls, from sorrow's stress,
Thy heart has never known recoil.

The cup of water given for thee
Still holds the freshness of thy grace;
Yet long these multitudes to see
The sweet compassion of thy face.

O Master, from the mountainside,
Make haste to heal these hearts of pain;
Among these restless throngs abide,
O tread the city's streets again.

Till all the world shall learn thy love,
And follow where thy feet have trod;
Till glorious from thy heaven above
Shall come the city of our God.

# A Mighty Fortress Is Our God

Martin Luther (1529)                          8.7.8.7.6.6.6.6.7
Trans. Frederick Henry Hedge (1852)                  Psalm 46

A mighty fortress is our God,
A bulwark never failing;
Our helper he amid the flood
Of mortal ills prevailing.
For still our ancient foe
Doth seek to work us woe;
His craft and power are great,
And, armed with cruel hate,
On earth is not his equal.

Did we in our own strength confide,
Our striving would be losing;
Were not the right Man on our side,
The Man of God's own choosing.
Dost ask who that may be?
Christ Jesus, it is he,
Lord Sabaoth his name,
From age to age the same,
And he must win the battle.

And though this world, with devils filled,
Should threaten to undo us,
We will not fear, for God hath willed
His truth to triumph through us.
The prince of darkness grim,
We tremble not for him;
His rage we can endure,
For lo! his doom is sure,
One little word shall fell him.

(*continued*)

That word above all earthly powers,
No thanks to them, abideth;
The Spirit and the gifts are ours
Through him who with us sideth;
Let goods and kindred go,
This mortal life also;
The body they may kill,
God's truth abideth still,
His kingdom is forever.

# God Is Working His Purpose Out

Arthur Campbell Ainger (1894)

God is working his purpose out
As year succeeds to year;
God is working his purpose out,
And the time is drawing near;
Nearer and nearer draws the time,
The time that shall surely be,
When the earth shall be filled with the glory of God
As the waters cover the sea.

From utmost east to utmost west,
Where'er man's foot hath trod,
By the mouth of many messengers
Goes forth the voice of God:
"Give ear to me, ye continents,
Ye isles, give ear to me,"
That the earth may be filled with the glory of God
As the waters cover the sea.

March we forth in the strength of God,
With the banner of Christ unfurled,
That the light of the glorious gospel of truth
May shine throughout the world:
Fight we the fight with sorrow and sin
To set their captives free,
That the earth may be filled with the glory of God
As the waters cover the sea.

All we can do is nothing worth
Unless God blesses the deed;
Vainly we hope for the harvesttide
Till God gives life to the seed;
Yet nearer and nearer draws the time,
The time that shall surely be,
When the earth shall be filled with the glory of God
As the waters cover the sea.

# All My Hope on God Is Founded

Joachim Neander (1680)                              8.7.8.7.6.7
Trans. Robert Seymour Bridges (1898)

All my hope on God is founded;
He doth still my trust renew.
Me through change and chance he guideth,
Only good and only true.
God unknown, he alone
Calls my heart to be his own.

Human pride and earthly glory,
Sword and crown betray his trust.
What with care and toil we fashion,
Tower and temple, fall to dust.
But God's power, hour by hour,
Is my temple and my tower.

God's great goodness e'er endureth;
Deep his wisdom, passing thought.
Splendor, light, and life attend him;
Beauty springeth out of nought.
Evermore from his store
Newborn worlds rise and adore.

Daily doth the almighty Giver
Bounteous gifts on us bestow;
His desire our soul delighteth;
Pleasure leads us where we go.
Love doth stand at his hand;
Joy doth wait on his command.

Still from earth to God eternal
Sacrifice of praise be done,
High above all praises praising
For the gift of Christ his Son.
Christ doth call one and all;
Ye who follow shall not fall.

## If God Himself Be for Me

Paul Gerhardt (1656)                                    7.6.7.6 D
Trans. Richard Massie (1857), adapt.                    Romans 8:31–39

If God himself be for me,
I may a host defy;
For when I pray, before me
My foes, confounded, fly.
If Christ, my Head and Master,
Befriend me from above,
What foe or what disaster
Can drive me from his love?

I build on this foundation,
That Jesus and his blood
Alone are my salvation,
The true, eternal good.
Without him all that pleases
Will vain and empty prove.
The gifts I have from Jesus
Alone are worth my love.

*(continued)*

Christ Jesus is my splendor,
My sun, my light, alone;
Were he not my defender
Before God's awesome throne,
I never should find favor
And mercy in his sight,
But be destroyed forever
As darkness by the light.

For joy my heart is ringing;
All sorrow disappears;
And full of mirth and singing,
It wipes away all tears.
The sun that cheers my spirit
Is Jesus Christ, my King;
The heaven I shall inherit
Makes me rejoice and sing.

## Jesus, Lover of My Soul

Charles Wesley (1740)                                    7.7.7.7 D

Jesus, lover of my soul,
Let me to thy bosom fly,
While the nearer waters roll,
While the tempest still is high:
Hide me, O my Savior, hide,
Till the storm of life is past;
Safe into the haven guide;
O receive my soul at last!

Other refuge have I none;
Hangs my helpless soul on thee;
Leave, ah! leave me not alone,
Still support and comfort me.
All my trust on thee is stayed,
All my help from thee I bring;
Cover my defenseless head
With the shadow of thy wing.

Thou, O Christ, art all I want;
More than all in thee I find:
Raise the fallen, cheer the faint,
Heal the sick, and lead the blind.
Just and holy is thy name;
I am all unrighteousness;
False and full of sin I am,
Thou art full of truth and grace.

Plenteous grace with thee is found,
Grace to cover all my sin;
Let the healing streams abound;
Make and keep me pure within.
Thou of life the fountain art,
Freely let me take of thee;
Spring thou up within my heart,
Rise to all eternity.

# Jesus, Lead the Way

Nicolaus L. von Zinzendorf (1721)                    5.5.8.8.5.5
Christian Gregor (1776)
Trans. Arthur William Farlander (1939)

Jesus, lead the way
Through our life's long day,
And with faithful footstep steady,
We will follow, ever ready.
Guide us by thy hand
To the Fatherland.

Should our lot be hard,
Keep us on our guard;
Even through severest trial
Make us brave in self-denial:
Transient pain may be
But a way to thee.

When we need relief
From an inner grief,
Or when evils come alluring,
Make us patient and enduring:
Let us follow still
Thy most holy will.

Order thou our ways,
Savior, all our days.
If thou lead us through rough places,
Grant us thy sustaining graces.
When our course is o'er,
Open heaven's door.

# Jesus, Priceless Treasure

Johann Franck (1650)                    6.6.5.6.6.5.7.8.6
Trans. Catherine Winkworth (1863)

Jesus, priceless treasure,
Source of purest pleasure,
Truest friend to me;
Long my heart hath panted,
Till it well-nigh fainted,
Thirsting after thee.
Thine I am, O spotless Lamb,
I will suffer nought to hide thee,
Ask for nought beside thee.

In thine arm I rest me;
Foes who would oppress me
Cannot reach me here.
Though the earth be shaking,
Every heart be quaking,
God dispels our fear;
Sin and hell in conflict fell
With their heaviest storms assail us:
Jesus will not fail us.

Hence, all thoughts of sadness!
For the Lord of gladness,
Jesus, enters in:
Those who love the Father,
Though the storms may gather,
Still have peace within;
Yea, whate'er we here must bear,
Still in thee lies purest pleasure,
Jesus, priceless treasure!

# Lord, When I Stand, No Path before Me Clear

T. Herbert O'Driscoll (1980)                                    10.10.10.10

Lord, when I stand, no path before me clear,
When every prayer seems prisoner of my pain,
Come with a gentleness which calms my fear,
Lord of my helplessness, my victory gain.

When all my prayers no answer seem to bring,
And there is silence in my deepest soul,
When in the wilderness I find no spring,
Lord of the desert places, keep me whole.

When the dark lord of loneliness prevails,
And, all defeated, joy and friendship die,
Come, be my joy, such love that never fails,
Pierce the self-pity of my shadowed sky.

When, as did Thomas, I presume thee dead,
Feeling and faith itself within me cold,
Freshen my lips with wine, my soul with bread,
Banish my poverty with heaven's gold.

# O Day of Peace

Carl P. Daw, Jr. (1982)

LMD
Isaiah 11:6–9

O day of peace that dimly shines
Through all our hopes and prayers and dreams,
Guide us to justice, truth, and love,
Delivered from our selfish schemes.
May swords of hate fall from our hands,
Our hearts from envy find release,
Till by God's grace our warring world
Shall see Christ's promised reign of peace.

Then shall the wolf dwell with the lamb,
Nor shall the fierce devour the small;
As beasts and cattle calmly graze,
A little child shall lead them all.
Then enemies shall learn to love,
All creatures find their true accord;
The hope of peace shall be fulfilled,
For all the earth shall know the Lord.

# O Love That Wilt Not Let Me Go

George Matheson (1882)                    8.8.8.8.6

O love that wilt not let me go,
I rest my weary soul in thee;
I give thee back the life I owe,
That in thine ocean depths its flow
May richer, fuller be.

O light that followest all my way,
I yield my flickering torch to thee;
My heart restores its borrowed ray,
That in thy sunshine's blaze its day
May brighter, fairer be.

O joy that seekest me through pain,
I cannot close my heart to thee;
I trace the rainbow through the rain,
And feel the promise is not vain
That morn shall tearless be.

O cross that liftest up my head,
I dare not ask to fly from thee;
I lay in dust life's glory dead,
And from the ground there blossoms red
Life that shall endless be.

## Our God, Our Help in Ages Past

Isaac Watts (1719)                                                        CM

Psalm 90:1–5

Our God, our help in ages past,
Our hope for years to come,
Our shelter from the stormy blast,
And our eternal home:

Before the hills in order stood,
Or earth received its frame,
From everlasting thou art God,
To endless years the same.

A thousand ages in thy sight
Are like an evening gone;
Short as the watch that ends the night
Before the rising sun.

Time, like an ever rolling stream,
Soon bears us all away;
We fly forgotten, as a dream
Dies at the opening day.

Our God, our help in ages past,
Our hope for years to come,
Be thou our guard while life shall last,
And our eternal home.

# Through the Night of Doubt and Sorrow

Bernard Severin Ingemann (1825)                    8.7.8.7 D
Trans. Sabine Baring-Gould (1867)

Through the night of doubt and sorrow
Onward goes the pilgrim band,
Singing songs of expectation,
Marching to the promised land.
Clear before us through the darkness
Gleams and burns the guiding light:
Trusting God we march together,
Stepping fearless through the night.

One the light of God's own presence,
O'er his ransomed people shed,
Chasing far the gloom and terror,
Brightening all the path we tread:
One the object of our journey,
One the faith which never tires,
One the earnest looking forward,
One the hope our God inspires.

One the strain the lips of thousands
Lift as from the heart of one;
One the conflict, one the peril,
One the march in God begun:
One the gladness of rejoicing
On the far eternal shore,
Where the one almighty Father
Reigns in love for evermore.

# Greet Now the Swiftly Changing Year

Slovak (1636)                                    8.8.8.6
Trans. Jaroslav J. Vajda (1958)

Greet now the swiftly changing year
With joy and penitence sincere.
Rejoice! Rejoice! With thanks embrace
Another year of grace.

Remember now the Son of God
And how he shed for us his blood.
Rejoice! Rejoice! With thanks embrace
Another year of grace.

This Jesus came to end sin's war;
This name of names for us he bore.
Rejoice! Rejoice! With thanks embrace
Another year of grace.

His love abundant far exceeds
The volume of a whole year's needs.
Rejoice! Rejoice! With thanks embrace
Another year of grace.

With him as Lord to lead our way
In want and in prosperity,
What need we fear in earth or space
In this new year of grace!

*(continued)*

"All glory be to God on high,
And peace on earth!" the angels cry.
Rejoice! Rejoice! With thanks embrace
Another year of grace.

God, Father, Son, and Spirit, hear!
To all our pleas incline your ear;
Upon our lives rich blessing trace
In this new year of grace.

## Lord of Our Growing Years

David Mowbray (1982)                                    6.6.6.6.8.8

Lord of our growing years,
With us from infancy,
Laughter and quick-dried tears,
Freshness and energy:
    Your grace surrounds us all our days;
    For all your gifts we bring our praise.

Lord of our strongest years,
Stretching our youthful powers,
Lovers and pioneers
When all the world seems ours:
    Your grace surrounds us all our days;
    For all your gifts we bring our praise.

Lord of our middle years,
Giver of steadfastness,
Courage that perseveres
When there is small success:
Your grace surrounds us all our days;
For all your gifts we bring our praise.

Lord of our older years,
Steep though the road may be,
Rid us of foolish fears,
Bring us serenity:
Your grace surrounds us all our days;
For all your gifts we bring our praise.

Lord of our closing years,
Always your promise stands;
Hold us, when death appears,
Safely within your hands:
Your grace surrounds us all our days;
For all your gifts we bring our praise.

# O Day of Rest and Gladness

Christopher Wordsworth (1862)                    7.6.7.6 D

O day of rest and gladness,
O day of joy and light,
O balm of care and sadness,
Most beautiful, most bright!
On thee the high and lowly,
Before the eternal throne,
Sing, "Holy, holy, holy,"
To the great Three in One.

On thee, at the creation,
The light first had its birth;
On thee, for our salvation,
Christ rose from depths of earth;
On thee our Lord victorious
The Spirit sent from heaven,
And thus on thee, most glorious,
A triple light was given.

Today on weary nations
The heavenly manna falls;
To holy convocations
The silver trumpet calls,
Where gospel light is glowing
With pure and radiant beams,
And living water flowing
With soul-refreshing streams.

New graces ever gaining
From this our day of rest,
We reach the rest remaining
To spirits of the blest.
To Holy Ghost be praises,
To Father, and to Son;
The church her voice upraises
To thee, blest Three in One.

## Now Praise the Hidden God of Love

Fred Pratt Green (1975)                                    LM

Now praise the hidden God of love,
In whom we all must live and move,
Who shepherds us at every stage,
Through youth, maturity, and age:

Who challenged us, when we were young,
To storm the citadels of wrong;
In care for others taught us how
God's true community must grow:

Who bids us never lose our zest,
Though age is urging us to rest,
But proves to us that we have still
A work to do, a place to fill.

# Awake, My Soul, and with the Sun

Thomas Ken (1674)                                          LM

Awake, my soul, and with the sun
Thy daily stage of duty run;
Shake off dull sloth, and joyful rise
To pay thy morning sacrifice.

Redeem thy misspent moments past;
And live this day as if thy last:
Improve thy talent with due care;
For the great day thyself prepare.

Let all thy converse be sincere,
Thy conscience as the noonday clear;
Think how all-seeing God thy ways
And all thy secret thoughts surveys.

Wake, and lift up thyself, my heart,
And with the angels bear thy part,
Who all night long unwearied sing
High praise to the eternal King.

All praise to thee, who safe hast kept
And hast refreshed me while I slept;
Grant, Lord, when I from death shall wake,
I may of endless light partake.

Lord, I my vows to thee renew;
Disperse my sins as morning dew;
Guard my first springs of thought and will,
And with thyself my spirit fill.

Direct, control, suggest, this day,
All I design, or do, or say;
That all my powers, with all their might,
In thy sole glory may unite.

Praise God, from whom all blessings flow;
Praise him, all creatures here below;
Praise him above, ye heavenly host:
Praise Father, Son, and Holy Ghost.

## Father, We Praise Thee

Latin (11th cent.)                              11.11.11.5
Trans. Percy Dearmer (1906)

Father, we praise thee, now the night is over;
Active and watchful, stand we all before thee;
Singing, we offer prayer and meditation:
Thus we adore thee.

Monarch of all things, fit us for thy mansions;
Banish our weakness, health and wholeness sending;
Bring us to heaven, where thy saints united
Joy without ending.

All-holy Father, Son, and equal Spirit,
Trinity blessed, send us thy salvation;
Thine is the glory, gleaming and resounding
Through all creation.

# O Splendor of God's Glory Bright

Ambrose of Milan (4th cent.)                                        LM
Trans. Robert Seymour Bridges (1899)

O Splendor of God's glory bright,
O thou who bringest light from light,
O Light of light, light's living spring,
O Day, all days illumining!

O thou true Sun, on us thy glance
Let fall in royal radiance;
The Spirit's sanctifying beam
Upon our earthly senses stream.

The Father, too, our prayers implore,
Father of glory evermore,
The Father of all grace and might,
To banish sin from our delight.

To guide whate'er we nobly do,
With love all envy to subdue,
To make ill-fortune turn to fair,
And give us grace our wrongs to bear.

Rejoicing may this day go hence;
Like virgin dawn our innocence,
Like fiery noon our faith appear,
Nor know the gloom of twilight drear.

Morn in her rosy car is borne;
Let him come forth, our perfect morn,
The Word in God the Father one,
The Father perfect in the Son.

All laud to God the Father be;
All praise, eternal Son, to thee;
All glory, as is ever meet,
To God the holy Paraclete.

## Christ, Whose Glory Fills the Skies

Charles Wesley (1740)                           7.7.7.7.7.7

Christ, whose glory fills the skies,
Christ, the true, the only light,
Sun of Righteousness, arise,
Triumph o'er the shades of night;
Dayspring from on high, be near;
Daystar, in my heart appear.

Dark and cheerless is the morn
Unaccompanied by thee;
Joyless is the day's return
Till thy mercy's beams I see,
Till they inward light impart,
Cheer my eyes and warm my heart.

Visit then this soul of mine;
Pierce the gloom of sin and grief;
Fill me, radiancy divine;
Scatter all my unbelief;
More and more thyself display,
Shining to the perfect day.

# When Morning Gilds the Skies

German (early 19th cent.)  6.6.6 D
Trans. Robert Seymour Bridges (1899)

When morning gilds the skies,
My heart awaking cries,
May Jesus Christ be praised!
When evening shadows fall,
This rings my curfew call:
May Jesus Christ be praised!

When mirth for music longs,
This is my song of songs:
May Jesus Christ be praised!
God's holy house of prayer
Hath none that can compare
With "Jesus Christ be praised!"

No lovelier antiphon
In all high heaven is known
Than "Jesus Christ be praised!"
There to the eternal Word
The eternal psalm is heard:
May Jesus Christ be praised!

Ye nations of mankind,
In this your concord find:
May Jesus Christ be praised!
Let all the earth around
Ring joyous with the sound:
May Jesus Christ be praised!

Sing, suns and stars of space,
Sing, ye that see his face,
Sing, Jesus Christ be praised!
God's whole creation o'er,
Both now and evermore,
Shall Jesus Christ be praised!

# O Gladsome Light

Greek (3d cent.)                                    6.6.7.6.6.7
Trans. Robert Seymour Bridges (1899)          *Phos hilaron*

O gladsome light, O grace
Of our Creator's face,
The eternal splendor wearing:
Celestial, holy, blest,
Our Savior Jesus Christ,
Joyful in your appearing.

As fades the day's last light,
We see the lamps of night
Our common hymn outpouring;
O God of might unknown,
You, the incarnate Son,
And Spirit blest adoring.

To you of right belongs
All praise of holy songs,
O Son of God, Life-giver;
You, therefore, O Most High,
The world does glorify
And shall exalt forever.

# Abide with Me

Henry Francis Lyte (1847)                                        10.10.10.10

Abide with me: fast falls the eventide;
The darkness deepens; Lord, with me abide!
When other helpers fail and comforts flee,
Help of the helpless, O abide with me.

Swift to its close ebbs out life's little day;
Earth's joys grow dim, its glories pass away;
Change and decay in all around I see.
O thou who changest not, abide with me.

I need thy presence every passing hour;
What but thy grace can foil the tempter's power?
Who, like thyself, my guide and stay can be?
Through cloud and sunshine, Lord, abide with me.

I fear no foe, with thee at hand to bless:
Ills have no weight, and tears no bitterness.
Where is death's sting? Where, grave, thy victory?
I triumph still, if thou abide with me.

Hold thou thy cross before my closing eyes;
Shine through the gloom and point me to the skies:
Heaven's morning breaks, and earth's vain shadows flee;
In life, in death, O Lord, abide with me.

# All Praise to Thee, My God, This Night

Thomas Ken (1674)                                    LM

All praise to thee, my God, this night,
For all the blessings of the light:
Keep me, O keep me, King of kings,
Beneath thine own almighty wings.

Forgive me, Lord, for thy dear Son,
The ill that I this day have done;
That with the world, myself, and thee,
I, ere I sleep, at peace may be.

Teach me to live, that I may dread
The grave as little as my bed;
Teach me to die, that so I may
Rise glorious at the awesome day.

O may my soul on thee repose,
And with sweet sleep mine eyelids close;
Sleep that shall me more vigorous make
To serve my God when I awake.

Praise God, from whom all blessings flow;
Praise him, all creatures here below;
Praise him above, ye heavenly host:
Praise Father, Son, and Holy Ghost.

## God, Who Made the Earth and Heaven

St. 1, Reginald Heber (publ. 1827)        8.4.8.4.8.8.8.4
Sts. 2, 4, William Mercer (1864)
St. 3, Richard Whately (1838)

God, who made the earth and heaven,
Darkness and light:
You the day for work have given,
For rest the night.
May your angel guards defend us,
Slumber sweet your mercy send us,
Holy dreams and hopes attend us
All through the night.

And, when morn again shall call us
To run life's way,
May we still, whate'er befall us,
Your will obey.
From the power of evil hide us,
In the narrow pathway guide us,
Never be your smile denied us
All through the day.

Guard us waking, guard us sleeping,
And, when we die,
May we in your mighty keeping
All peaceful lie.
When the last dread call shall wake us,
Then, O Lord, do not forsake us,
But to reign in glory take us
With you on high.

Holy Father, throned in heaven,
All-holy Son,
Holy Spirit, freely given,
Blest Three in One:
Grant us grace, we now implore you,
Till we lay our crowns before you
And in worthier strains adore you
While ages run.

# The Day Thou Gavest, Lord, Is Ended

John Ellerton (1870)　　　　　　　　　　　　　　　　9.8.9.8

The day thou gavest, Lord, is ended,
The darkness falls at thy behest;
To thee our morning hymns ascended,
Thy praise shall hallow now our rest.

We thank thee that thy church unsleeping,
While earth rolls onward into light,
Through all the world a watch is keeping
And rests not now by day or night.

As o'er each continent and island
The dawn leads on another day,
The voice of prayer is never silent,
Nor dies the strain of praise away.

The sun that bids us rest is waking
Thy children 'neath the western sky,
And hour by hour fresh lips are making
Thy wondrous doings heard on high.

So be it, Lord; thy throne shall never,
Like earth's proud empires, pass away;
Thy kingdom stands, and grows forever
Till all thy creatures own thy sway.

# Day of Judgment! Day of Wonders!

Latin (13th cent.)
8.7.8.7.4.7
Trans. and para. John Newton (1774)
*Dies irae, dies illa*

Day of judgment! Day of wonders!
Hark! the trumpet's awesome sound,
Louder than a thousand thunders,
Shakes the vast creation round.
How the summons
Will the sinner's heart confound!

See the Judge, our nature wearing,
Clothed in majesty divine.
You who long for his appearing
Then shall say, "This God is mine!"
Gracious Savior,
Own me on that day as thine.

At his call the dead awaken,
Rise to life from earth and sea.
All the powers of nature, shaken
By his looks, prepare to flee.
Careless sinner,
What will then become of thee?

But to those who have confessèd,
Loved, and served the Lord below,
He will say, "Come near, you blessèd,
See the kingdom I bestow;
You forever
Shall my love and glory know."

# Jerusalem the Golden

Bernard of Cluny (12th cent.)                    7.6.7.6 D
Trans. John Mason Neale (1851)

Jerusalem the golden,
With milk and honey blest,
Beneath thy contemplation
Sink heart and voice oppressed:
I know not, O I know not,
What joys await us there;
What radiancy of glory,
What bliss beyond compare!

They stand, those halls of Zion,
All jubilant with song,
And bright with many an angel,
And all the martyr throng:
The Prince is ever in them,
The daylight is serene;
The pastures of the blessèd
Are decked in glorious sheen.

There is the throne of David;
And there, from care released,
The shout of them that triumph,
The song of them that feast;
And they who with their Leader
Have conquered in the fight,
Forever and forever
Are clad in robes of white.

O sweet and blessèd country,
The home of God's elect!
O sweet and blessèd country
That eager hearts expect!
Jesus, in mercy bring us
To that dear land of rest,
Who art, with God the Father,
And Spirit, ever blest.

# Here from All Nations

Christopher Idle (1973)                                    11.10.11.10
                                                   Revelation 7:9–17

Here from all nations, all tongues, and all peoples,
Countless the crowd but their voices are one.
Vast is the sight and majestic their singing:
"God has the victory: He reigns from the throne!"

These have come out of the great tribulation;
Now they may stand in the presence of God,
Serving their Lord day and night in his temple,
Ransomed and cleansed by the Lamb's precious blood.

Gone is their thirst and no more shall they hunger;
God is their shelter, his power at their side.
Sun shall not pain them, no burning will torture;
Jesus the Lamb is their shepherd and guide.

He will go with them to clear living water
Flowing from springs which his mercy supplies.
Gone is their grief, and their trials are over.
God wipes away every tear from their eyes.

Blessing and glory and wisdom and power
Be to the Savior again and again,
Might and thanksgiving and honor forever
Be to our God: Alleluia! Amen.

# For All the Saints

William Walsham How (1864)                              10.10.10 Alleluias

For all the saints who from their labors rest,
Who thee by faith before the world confessed,
Thy name, O Jesus, be forever blest.
Alleluia! Alleluia!

Thou wast their rock, their fortress, and their might;
Thou, Lord, their captain in the well-fought fight;
Thou, in the darkness drear, their one true light.
Alleluia! Alleluia!

O may thy soldiers, faithful, true, and bold,
Fight as the saints who nobly fought of old,
And win with them the victor's crown of gold.
Alleluia! Alleluia!

O blest communion, fellowship divine!
We feebly struggle, they in glory shine;
Yet all are one in Thee, for all are thine.
Alleluia! Alleluia!

And when the strife is fierce, the warfare long,
Steals on the ear the distant triumph song,
And hearts are brave again, and arms are strong.
Alleluia! Alleluia!

From earth's wide bounds, from ocean's farthest coast,
Through gates of pearl streams in the countless host,
Singing to Father, Son, and Holy Ghost,
Alleluia! Alleluia!

# Look, Ye Saints, the Sight Is Glorious

Thomas Kelly (1809)                                      8.7.8.7.4.7

Look, ye saints, the sight is glorious;
See the Man of Sorrows now;
From the fight returned victorious,
Every knee to him shall bow:
Crown him! crown him!
Crowns become the victor's brow.

Crown the Savior, angels, crown him;
Rich the trophies Jesus brings;
In the seat of power enthrone him,
While the vault of heaven rings;
Crown him! crown him!
Crown the Savior King of kings.

Sinners in derision crowned him,
Mocking thus Messiah's claim;
Saints and angels throng around him,
Own his title, praise his name;
Crown him! crown him!
Spread abroad the victor's fame!

Hark! those bursts of acclamation!
Hark! those loud triumphant chords!
Jesus takes the highest station;
O what joy the sight affords!
Crown him! crown him!
King of kings and Lord of lords.

# Jesus Christ, My Sure Defense

Anon. German (1653)                                         7.8.7.8.7.7
Trans. based on Catherine Winkworth (1863)

Jesus Christ, my sure defense
And my Savior, ever liveth;
Knowing this, my confidence
Rests upon the hope it giveth
Though the night of death be fraught
Still with many an anxious thought.

Jesus, my Redeemer, lives;
I, too, unto life shall waken.
Endless joy my Savior gives;
Shall my courage, then, be shaken?
Shall I fear, or could the Head
Rise and leave his members dead?

Nay, too closely am I bound
Unto him by hope forever;
Faith's strong hand the Rock hath found,
Grasped it, and will leave it never;
Even death now cannot part
From its Lord the trusting heart.

I am flesh and must return
Unto dust, whence I am taken;
But by faith I now discern
That from death I shall awaken
With my Savior to abide
In his glory, at his side.

*(continued)*

295

Glorified, I shall anew
With this flesh then be enshrouded;
In this body I shall view
God, my Lord, with eyes unclouded;
In this flesh I then shall see
Jesus Christ eternally.

Then these eyes my Lord shall know,
My Redeemer and my Brother;
In his love my soul shall glow,
I myself, and not another!
Then the weakness I feel here
Shall forever disappear.

They who sorrow here and moan
There in gladness shall be reigning;
Earthly here the seed is sown,
There immortal life attaining.
Here our sinful bodies die,
Glorified to dwell on high.

Then take comfort and rejoice,
For his members Christ will cherish.
Fear not, they will hear his voice,
Dying, they shall never perish;
For the very grave is stirred
When the trumpet's blast is heard.

Laugh to scorn the gloomy grave
And at death no longer tremble;
He, the Lord, who came to save
Will at last his own assemble.
They will go their Lord to meet,
Treading death beneath their feet.

O, then, draw away your hearts
Now from pleasures base and hollow.
There to share what he imparts.
Here his footsteps ye must follow.
Fix your hearts beyond the skies,
Whither ye yourselves would rise.

## Even as We Live Each Day

Martin Luther (1524)
Trans. composite

Even as we live each day,
Death our life embraces.
Who is there to bring us help,
Rich, forgiving graces?
You only, Lord, you only!
Baptized in Christ's life-giving flood:
Water and his precious blood—
Holy and righteous God,
Holy and mighty God,
Holy and all-merciful Savior,
Everlasting God,
By grace bring us safely
Through the flood of bitter death.
Lord, have mercy.

# O Holy City, Seen of John

Walter Russell Bowie (1909)                              8.6.8.6.8.6

O holy city, seen of John,
Where Christ, the Lamb, does reign,
Within whose foursquare walls shall come
No night, nor need, nor pain,
And where the tears are wiped from eyes
That shall not weep again!

O shame to us who rest content
While lust and greed for gain
In street and shop and tenement
Wring gold from human pain,
And bitter lips in blind despair
Cry, "Christ has died in vain!"

Give us, O God, the strength to build
The city that has stood
Too long a dream, whose laws are love,
Whose ways are servanthood,
And where the sun that shines becomes
God's grace for human good.

Already in the mind of God
That city rises fair.
Lo, how its splendor challenges
The souls that greatly dare,
And bids us seize the whole of life
And build its glory there.

# Index of Authors, Translators, and Sources

# Index of First Lines and Titles